SECRETS OF SUCCESS
North Carolina Values-Based Leadership

SECRETS OF SUCCESS
North Carolina Values-Based Leadership

General H. Hugh Shelton Leadership Center
NC State University
General H. Hugh Shelton
United States Army (R)
14th Chairman, Joint Chiefs of Staff

Photographs by Simon Griffiths

PUBLISHED BY IVY HOUSE PUBLISHING GROUP
5122 Bur Oak Circle, Raleigh, NC 27612 USA
919-782-0281
www.ivyhousebooks.com

Cover Images from BigStockPhoto.com

Bald Eagle, 2008 © Rob Cocquyt. Dawn On the Lake, 2008 © Angela Keane.

ISBN13: 978-1-57197-495-2
Library of Congress Control Number: 2008941754

Printed in the United States of America

Contents

Acknowledgments

My thanks to the leadership of North Carolina State University—James L. Oblinger, Chancellor; Johnny Wynne, Dean of the College of Agriculture and Life Sciences; Keith Oakley, President of The North Carolina Agricultural Foundation, Inc.; James Zuiches, Vice Chancellor, Extension, Engagement, and Economic Development; Mike Davis, Director, General H. Hugh Shelton Leadership Center; Debbie Reno, Coordinator of Educational Programs and Training; and David Hays, who serves as my Special Assistant at the Center.

It was the leadership from The North Carolina Agricultural Foundation, Inc. that also made this a reality. The financial support of Chris Collins and John McNeill enabled us to take this project to publication. Chris and John, we thank you. Thanks are also due to Stuart and Tabetha Cooke for their generous contribution and early buy-in to this project.

Thanks to Bob Cairns for the concept, research, and interviews and to Simon Griffiths for his incredible photography. Also thanks go to Simon's assistants Rick Ward and Amber Gerberich. I'd be remiss if I didn't mention June Brotherton for her project management skills. Alyce Cairns provided early editing. Julia Brooks offered important clerical and budget management support. Bob Milks did a splendid job of editing the copy. My heartfelt thanks to Greg Miller for his excellent design work—the cover and the pages

herein. And to *NC State*, my alumni magazine, where the Kay Yow interview, as told to Cherry Crayton, first appeared in the spring 2007 issue. A special thank-you to Becky Bumgardner for her help. Scott Troutman, Jim Kelley, Kathy Kennel, and Pam Byington proved to be important first readers and advisors to the project. Thanks to my wife, Carolyn, whose numerous suggestions proved invaluable to the final product. The support of the Board of Advisors of the Leadership Center is greatly appreciated.

A special thank-you to UNC President Emeritus William C. Friday for his brilliant foreword, an essay that goes to the core concept of leadership. He and the leaders who follow are the secrets of this book's success. Thank you, one and all, for your generosity, time, talent, expertise, and unique insights into leadership: Herman Boone, subject of the film *Remember the Titans*; Erskine Bowles, President, The University of North Carolina; Colonel Curtis L. Brown, Jr., U.S. Air Force (R), former NASA astronaut; Julius L. Chambers, North Carolina civil-rights attorney; Donna Chavis, Executive Director, NCGives; Dr. T. Ming Chu, former Director of cancer research at Roswell Park Cancer Institute, the State University of New York at Buffalo; Dr. Johnnetta B. Cole, former President, Spelman College; Alan Dickson, the Ruddick Corporation and Harris Teeter; Bob Etheridge, U.S. Congressman; David Gergen, CNN political analyst

and former presidential adviser; Ann Goodnight, Director of community relations, SAS, and co-founder of Cary Academy; Dr. Catherine Gordon, Director, Harvard's Bone Health Program for Children, Children's Hospital Boston; Edward M. Gore, Sr., real estate developer; Franklin Graham, CEO, Samaritan's Purse; William Harrison, former Chairman and CEO, JPMorgan Chase & Co.; Governor James E. Holshouser, Jr.; Governor James B. Hunt, Jr.; Jeanette W. Hyde, former Ambassador to seven Caribbean countries; Hugh McColl, Jr., former CEO, Bank of America; General Dan K. McNeill, U.S. Army (R); Dr. Carmaleta Littlejohn Monteith, North Carolina educator; David H. Murdock, President, Dole Foods and Castle & Cooke, Inc.; Wendell Murphy, Chairman Emeritus, Murphy Family Ventures, LLC; Arnold Palmer, Arnold Palmer Enterprises; Richard Petty, "Founding Father," Victory Junction Gang Camp for Kids; Dr. Jerry Punch, ABC/ESPN NASCAR Commentator; Jerry Richardson, owner, Carolina Panthers; Charlie Rose, host of *Charlie Rose*; Mary Duke Biddle Trent Semans, supporter of education and arts programs across the Carolinas; Rear Admiral Ralph E. Suggs, U.S. Navy (R) and Harley-Davidson executive; Dr. LeRoy Walker, former Head, U.S. Olympic Committee; Tab Williams, Williams Oil; and Kay Yow, NC State University and U.S. Olympic Women's Basketball Coach.

I especially acknowledge the late Coach Yow whose death occurred as "Secrets of Success" was going to press. Her life's work and her courageous fight against cancer were inspirational to the original concept of this book.

Preface

When we established the General H. Hugh Shelton Leadership Center at North Carolina State University, our focus was clear. Our mission is to inspire, educate, and develop values-based leaders committed to personal integrity, professional ethics, and selfless service. As a young man, I was on an Edgecombe County 4-H livestock judging team, one of four sixteen-year-old members. We had just won the North Carolina state championship and were in Chicago to compete for the national championship. Problem: we learned that each member of the team had to be sixteen years of age by January 1. My birthday was January 2. We were devastated when we learned that we could only compete if we claimed my birthday to be January 1. Our coach, Mr. Charles Lockhart, laid out our options. We could withdraw or request a waiver, since to do otherwise would not be honest. We requested the waiver, and in the end, we were allowed to compete, as if eligible, although our scores wouldn't count in the final results. As it turned out, our scores were respectable but not quite good enough. So we didn't win the competition. But the leadership lesson I learned there was invaluable. It was a lesson about honesty and integrity that I never forgot, and that frankly, thanks to Mr. Lockhart, remained with me throughout my military career and later as we envisioned this leadership center here at NC State.

To support this leadership vision, we have created a number of outstanding programs. We sponsor a Leadership Forum engaging leaders from the corporate sector, K-12, higher education, and agency professionals—all in the pursuit of championing the importance of values-based leadership. The Center also engages the next generation through educational scholarships and enrichment experiences that encourage active learning in a global context.

We offer intensive, week-long summer leadership-development experiences for high school students focusing on what I consider to be five of the cornerstones of leadership—honesty, integrity, compassion, diversity, and social responsibility. So we started with a number of valuable initiatives in place to promote leadership; however, as the years passed, it occurred to us that there was a missing piece to our efforts. We had no intention of producing a textbook on leadership, for that is a road that has been well traveled. There are literally hundreds of books available with the word "leadership" in the titles. What we were searching for was a calling card for the Center, one that would demonstrate our mission in real life, one that would celebrate the legacy of values-based leaders. We found our answer in *Secrets of Success: North Carolina Values-Based Leadership*.

In this beautiful coffee-table book, you will hear the voices of some of the state's great leaders, people who have served North Carolina and our nation in a diversity of arenas—business, government, education, religion, the military, the arts, and athletics. Each anecdotal memory here sheds a unique light that clearly highlights values-based leadership. The brilliant black-and-white portraits of these leaders complement their thoughts; if you look carefully, you can literally see leadership in their eyes and faces.

As I reviewed their thoughts, it became instantly clear that this is a modest gathering, a fraternity of men and women who have found the secret to their own success in others, often their mothers, fathers, teachers, or mentors, people like Charles Lockhart. And it was no surprise that this is a well-grounded group, one whose lessons of leadership were learned—in most cases—on the playing fields of life through experience, education, and hard work.

Through their voices, you'll learn the role that mentors played in their lives and how they made them better leaders. Again, thirty-four voices, all sharing their unique and diverse views of values-based leadership—from David Gergen, who advised four presidents, to Julius Chambers, who led the fight to integrate North Carolina schools, to former U.S. Women's Olympic basketball coach Kay Yow and Dr. Johnnetta Cole, head of the Johnnetta B. Cole Global Diversity & Inclusion Institute. And although this feature was not by design, I find it quite fitting that all of our nation's military services are represented here—General Dan McNeill (R), U.S. Army; Rear Admiral Ralph E. Suggs (R), U.S. Navy; Colonel Curtis L. Brown, Jr. (R), U.S. Air Force; Hugh McColl, U.S. Marine Corps; and Arnold Palmer, who served in the U.S. Coast Guard. Over the years, I've been honored to speak on the subject of leadership on numerous occasions. The question that I receive most often is this: define values-based leadership. I have that definition. Values-based leadership is influencing others through the commitment to personal integrity, professional ethics, and selfless service. But that said, my answer has now become even more clearly defined. If asked today, I suggest taking a look at *Secrets of Success: North Carolina Values-Based Leadership*. The voices of these incredible leaders not only tell our Center's story, they define leadership in a most attractive and inherently readable way.

H. HUGH SHELTON
GENERAL, USA (R)
14th Chairman, Joint Chiefs of Staff

Foreword

The creation of the General H. Hugh Shelton Leadership Center and the good work flowing from the general's initiative dramatically focuses our attention on a major crisis in our country today—the hunger for creative, courageous leaders possessing the integrity that inspires public trust. I can think of no one who better personifies leadership than General Hugh Shelton. Rising to his nation's call as the fourteenth chairman of the Joint Chiefs of Staff, he is truly a great American, a role-model leader of the highest order. The fact that the General H. Hugh Shelton Leadership Center is based at our shared alma mater gives me a great deal of pride. Our university has produced some of this nation's great leaders. However, the fact that the leaders found here in *Secrets of Success* aren't limited to a single university, or to a single profession, makes this book all the more compelling.

The late John Gardner, former secretary of Health, Education and Welfare and the acknowledged authority on leadership, in his book *On Leadership* pointed out that leadership is not status, nor is it to be confused with power. It is not official authority. What qualities then mark the men and women in whom we place our trust when crises come? Dr. Gardner answers that question by pointing out that leaders are visionary. They think ahead. Leaders realize that the welfare, growth, and development of others measures their own effectiveness. They work hard. They value time, and humor is a part of their very being.

Compassion looms large in the lives of leaders and a keen sense of fairness motivates their decision making. As the Center for Creative Leadership mission states: "Leaders . . . possess the capacity to think and act beyond boundaries to achieve more than imagined." The leaders that I have known and those with whom I have worked have understood that truth and integrity are fundamentally essential in all aspects of their lives. These character hallmarks underpin the loyalty, support, and commitment of all others they seek to lead.

As you turn these pages of *Secrets of Success* you will examine these qualities in the lives of these splendid Americans. It was these qualities that brought LeRoy Walker from a family of eleven to be the first African American to head the U.S. Olympic Committee and to lead all Olympians through the opening ceremonies in his hometown of Atlanta. As you read about him and all the others, you will discover that in every aspect of their lives there is the flowering of the real meaning of our democratic society—you can be what you seek to be if you will seize the moment and responsibly strive for success. I would characterize this group as a hard-working lot, people who had, in most cases, mentors who taught them the value of honesty, modesty, and integrity. One of their great secrets of success, it would appear, is that they, to a person, all remember from whence they came.

The publication of *Secrets of Success* is both timely and most important in responding to our nation's great longing for leaders in whom they can place their trust, respect, and confidence. As we look about our country today we see great corporations being destroyed by fraud and greed and the lack of diligence by their officers. We see too much manufactured celebrity status being confused with leadership. The corruption of television with raw violence and vulgarity exceeding any rational standards threatens a generation of our children. And we have so abused public officials and candidates for public office that the lack of civility in our behavior has reached disgraceful dimensions and drives good people from public service.

This collection of biographical glimpses makes clear that it doesn't have to be this way in America. General Shelton is showing us that there is a better way and that it is our task, yours and mine, to rediscover and recommit ourselves to the ancient virtues of truth, integrity, compassion, trust, decency, civility, and service to others. If indeed we are to be the exemplary nation in this differing global neighborhood we must give primacy to these qualities of leadership among ourselves. Being people of faith and democratic in our government policies and in our relationship with others, we have no other choice. Indeed, we have no greater opportunity. We are challenged by these watchwords from my dear friend Erskine Bowles, "Leaders can't be afraid of failure. What we have to be is not afraid to try."

Thank you, General Shelton, for these individual stories. They inspire and motivate us toward greater personal commitment to fulfilling our public trust for building a meaningful future for generations yet to come.

WILLIAM C. FRIDAY
PRESIDENT EMERITUS
The University of North Carolina

Kay Yow

Keeping It in Perspective

Women's head basketball coach, North Carolina State University; as coach won Olympic gold twice; selected for enshrinement into the Women's Basketball Hall of Fame and the Naismith Memorial Basketball Hall of Fame; received the inaugural Jimmy V ESPY Award for Perseverance

I'll tell you a story about a leader. You never know when one will impact your life. When I was in high school the coaches were men, and the opportunity wasn't there, so I never really thought about coaching. I saw myself being a teacher. When I got out of college, I applied for a job at Allen Jay High School in High Point. The principal, Mr. A. Doyle Early, knew me when I was a player at Gibsonville. The Southern Association of Colleges and Schools was starting to accredit high schools, and they wanted a woman associated with their women's basketball team. A guy had

coached both the girls and boys for thirteen years there. And I was applying to teach senior English. Mr. Early wanted me to coach the girls. I thought, "No way." Basically, Mr. Early talked me into doing it.

Now, Mr. Early was a leader, a man who kept me crossing my t's, dotting my i's. I had to be on top of things because he had high expectations.

During my first year there, we won the regular season. It wasn't because of my coaching; it was because of some great players that were on that team. We ended up playing in the tournament championship, and the game went right down to the wire. We had a one-point lead, but the team we were playing—with about 12 seconds left—hit a shot that put them one point up. My players just took the ball out of bounds, passed it up the right side; another player ran up the left and across to the free throw line on the other end. We made two passes and hit this player—that was my best player—and she just went up in the air and shot. As she shot, time ran out. The ball hit the back of the rim and bounced straight up for what seemed like an eternity. When it came down, it swished through the net. We had won the championship. My players had towels in their hands, and they just threw the towels in the air. It was a great celebration, and everybody was coming over, shaking my hand, saying congratulations.

I was floating in the sky. I was in the clouds. This went on for about thirty minutes. Then I saw Mr. Early walking toward me. He was a man of few compliments. I thought, "Wow! He's coming up like everybody else to shake my hand and tell me 'Great job.' " As he got

closer, I noticed the expression on his face wasn't like everybody else's. I had my hand out, but I put it down. I was twenty-two, enjoying this moment tremendously, probably thinking more highly of myself than I ought to. He came over and said, "Coach Yow, you brought twelve towels over here, and I want you to take twelve towels back."

My feet just went bam. I came down out of the clouds. When he said something, he expected it to happen. And then he said, "You brought twelve towels. You need to count and make sure you have twelve towels to go back. Count the towels." Then he just left. Now stragglers were coming over to congratulate me, and I had to just say, "Well, thanks, but I've got something I have got to take care of." I had to start looking for those towels because I knew I either had to get them or buy more, because he would come by my homeroom on Monday to see if they were there. Mr. Early gave me a great lesson in perspective and leadership, one I'll never forget.

Leaders help others keep things in perspective. "OK, so you won. But you have responsibilities, and you are accountable for things, and you will have to be sure that those things are taken care of. You can't lose focus and lose track. It is a great win, but that is not the only thing happening out here." Even when I won the gold medal in the Olympics in Seoul in 1988, as the clock was ticking down in that final game, a marquee was going around in my head that just said, "Count the towels."

I think that most leaders have had a Mr. Early in their lives, someone who reminded them to keep things in perspective and no matter how big the wins or the losses, the successes or failures, to always remember to count those towels.

David Gergen

Early Leadership, Lasting Influence

Professor of public service and director of the Center for Public Leadership at the John F. Kennedy School of Government at Harvard University; senior political analyst for CNN and editor-at-large of U.S. News & World Report; served in the White House as adviser to four presidents

I've had the privilege of working with American presidents (Nixon, Ford, Reagan, and Clinton) and walking with kings. I once attended a session in the Vatican with the president and the pope where one of my favorite presidents, Ronald Reagan, dozed off.

But in truth, there were two leaders who were most formative in my growing-up years. Both were from North Carolina, and they taught me so much about leadership. Terry Sanford was a graduate of the University of North Carolina–Chapel Hill. David Coltrane was a graduate of North Carolina State. When I was in college, Terry Sanford was elected governor of the state. I grew up in Durham, went off to college in the Northeast (Yale University and the Harvard Law School), and during the summer I applied to be an intern in Raleigh with the Sanford administration. Terry Sanford was just a magnet to public service and, over the years, brought in a number of people whom I came to admire—Walter Dellinger, Bob Spearman, Dan Blue, and eventually, Jim Hunt.

I went to work for the Commerce Department, where they assigned me to do analysis for companies that were considering relocation in North Carolina. One of my first assignments was to figure out whether there was a market for a tire repair company. They sent me to some godforsaken lot outside Raleigh . . . this was in ninety-five degree heat, a sweltering day. My job was to count tires. The next day, knowing that there must be something better to do with my life, I called Joel Fleishman in Governor Sanford's office and said, "There's something that Governor Sanford is doing that I'd like to be involved in."

Terry, in his infinite wisdom, had established a North Carolina Good Neighbor Council to address the issues of civil rights. This was the early '60s. There were demonstrations across the South, explosions in various states, and a great fear of this unrest spreading to North Carolina. Terry was an enlightened leader, far ahead of his time, a man who believed that the way to deal with this was to take it head-on. The purpose of the Council was to help keep the peace by setting up biracial councils across the state. This would be the first time in North Carolina that whites and blacks would come together to focus on the issues of public education and jobs.

I was sent to the office of David Coltrane, a man who'd grown up in hardscrabble North Carolina. He'd gone to NC State, become a Kerr Scott Democrat, and was now Terry's budget director. He wore one of those green eyeshades, a smallish man who looked a little bit like Harry Truman. Coltrane had been a segregationist his entire life, someone who believed that this was the right system, the way things were and the way they should be. When I went to see him to apply, I learned that the North Carolina Good Neighbor Council was one secretary and David Coltrane. That was

it. I signed on as his intern for the summer, and we began turning out materials, handouts about the Council. Then we just started going around the state. I was his driver, "Driving Mr. David." What I discovered on those trips was that this man who had been a staunch believer in segregation in the latter part of his life had now come one hundred and eighty degrees—to the point where he believed that integration was right, that African Americans had been held back, and that peace in the state would only come by introducing racial progress and racial harmony. He was a convert, an advocate for this.

And David was someone that everybody trusted. They admired him for who he'd become and for his values. So he put those councils together for Terry and they worked extremely well. Because of this leadership, North Carolina was spared a lot of the racial violence that devastated other states. These councils helped bring down the walls between the races and helped the walls between the South and the rest of the country fall. It was now easier for North Carolina to join the economy of the rest of the nation.

Two very different men from different backgrounds—Terry Sanford, a leader of the New South, and David Coltrane, a leader willing to change, a man who converted to the New South. That was more than forty years ago. In the years that have passed, I've had the opportunity to work in the White House, the privilege of advising presidents and other leaders. But I look back at those days with Terry Sanford and David Coltrane as the most satisfying of my public life. I'm grateful to those two leaders who were so influential in my formative years. I'm enormously grateful for what their leadership did for the civil-rights movement and for the state of North Carolina.

IRON MIKE
IN HONOR OF
AIRBORNE TROOPS
WHOSE COURAGE
DEDICATION, AND
TRADITIONS MAKE
THE WORLD
FIGHTING

General Dan K. McNeill, USA (R)

Commanding an Alliance

Four-star general, U.S. Army (R);

commanded the International Security

Assistance Force, Afghanistan

I led a NATO command called International Security Assistance Force in Afghanistan, an outfit that has the responsibility for the security mandate that covers all of Afghanistan. This force includes forty countries acknowledged by NATO, plus several others. The leadership charge that I dealt with on a day-to-day basis included pursuing the insurgents, working with hundreds of millions of dollars applied to building schools and roads, increasing electricity, and managing agricultural products. And we are trying to do our piece, which is somewhat limited by mandate, in controlling one of the world's largest illicit opium operations, the poppy crops grown in Helmand Province. This is a very dysfunctional place and a great cause of the problems that exist in Afghanistan.

So we are there to help the Afghans reestablish what really isn't a failed state but one that's been destroyed by over thirty years of war. Commanding an alliance is both blessing and bane. It's good to have that many nations, to have the force that we have in that country. But what I've learned in commanding an alliance is that although these countries have committed to a common objective, they also have political constituents, and these national interests, more often than not, don't follow the collective interests. So we end up with forty-some odd nations not all willing to do what each of the others will do. That is, in a very succinct way, the biggest challenge that I faced in this leadership position.

I don't want to get into self-aggrandizement but before I took over, the headlines were replete with "NATO FAILING TO GET JOB DONE IN AFGHANISTAN." And it was only a few weeks after I got there that I realized, as we say in the military, that we were not giving weight together, pulling together as rowers might in a boat. The first thing I had to do was to make sure that everybody clearly understood how I saw the NATO mandate. We were going to help the Afghans rebuild their country mostly through our provincial reconstruction teams, help them give their governance some peace, and lastly, we were going to fight and go after the insurgents, which was what we were supposed to do. That seemed to be an anathema to some members of the alliance.

But I said, "Here are the orders, get outside of the wire and do this and do that," and they did. We started pushing hard in the north in the Helmand Province, and this created an explosion of negative reactions. So I had a very tough fight for several months with most of the countries in the alliance contending that everything was all right up there, when it wasn't. We continued to put the pressure on the insurgents, and finally when the (NATO) Council came to Afghanistan on one of its scheduled visits, I walked them through everything I was doing, what I was trying to do, and they understood. Everyone sort of got it. It was at that point that the alliance started building, going from 36,000 to better than 50,000 soldiers.

This was a question of a basic leadership premise: leadership is important in word and deed, and if you profess to be something that you're not, then the enemy will figure it out quicker than anybody else. You have to have a vision, you have to know where you want to go, and then you have to get everyone to buy into that plan. I had some tough days, but criticism comes with leadership, and so you have to follow that vision no matter what the naysayers say, stay the course.

Nobody gives leaders anything but opportunities, and along the way there have been leaders who have helped me and my career; Hugh Shelton's not the least of them. Each of these leaders showed me something, and one was that the most important thing you can be is painfully honest, the first time, every time, all the time. You must understand that you are a part of an organization and understand the mission of the organization, and you must produce. When those in command weren't offering this kind of leadership, I just said, "I can't be like that, I can't live that way and look at myself in the mirror." I was recently asked by a *Washington Post* reporter why things were going so much better with our counterinsurgency efforts in the U.S. sectors and I said, "Make no mistake about it, the United States Army is probably one of the finest learning institutions in the world." We're not what many people say we are, trained by leadership to be martinets and robotic. We are open-minded. If you remember Nipper, the RCA dog, looking at that record . . . well, we as military leaders wouldn't want him to be just amazed that his master's voice is coming out of the gramophone. We'd want him to be thinking, asking questions like, "How did you do that? How did you put that voice in there?"

Hugh McColl, Jr.

The Measure of a Marine

Transformed through acquisitions North Carolina National Bank—a small regional bank—into NationsBank and then Bank of America; served as chairman and chief executive officer of Bank of America Corporation which, upon his retirement, had $610 billion in assets, $352 billion in deposits, and $49 billion in shareholders equity; was the driving force behind the consolidation that characterizes the commercial banking industry today

I've been blessed with leadership skills, skills that were developed as an officer in the Marine Corps. I learned some very simple precepts, precepts that worked. If you're going to lead people, you have to do it from in front. You don't order people into battle, you lead them. So in business, if you wish to accomplish something, you lead by example. If you want your people to work late at night to meet a deadline, then you should be working with them. And the troops have to eat first. In a business sense, that means looking after your people first, see that they're paid well, treated properly.

The thing that I really learned in the Marine Corps, and this was a great change in my life, was that everybody pulled their pants on the same way. I'd grown up fairly privileged, went to the University of North Carolina–Chapel Hill, got in with no problem. I'd lived in a segregated society and, candidly, had not thought about this critically. In the Marine Corps, I learned that you judged a man on what he could do as opposed to who his parents were or where he went to school. So during my years at the helm at Bank of America, my leadership view was to judge people only on what they did, not on any other artificial criteria. Another thing the Marine Corps taught was that when you put on that uniform you were a marine. There were expectations of you as a marine.

So I adopted the same philosophy in my company. If you put on our uniform you were one of us, and we trusted you. An employee didn't have to prove to me that I could trust them, I already did. They could only prove to me that I shouldn't. I had a great team of people and we took a very small bank, NCNB, and built it into the largest bank in the United States. I used the walk-around management style. Memos weren't my thing. If someone wrote to me I wanted the punch line right up front. We communicated with all our employees personally and with the thousands who joined us during our acquisitions. I went out of my way to tell people what counted, what our expectations were. I encouraged open debates in the war room. Rank didn't matter—if you had a better opinion, it could carry the day. But once we made a decision, we came out of that room in lockstep. Then we went to the execution stage. Now I don't mean to say that I couldn't change my opinion or my direction. But if I did, it was only based on new and valuable information. I'd be a fool to say that everyone embraced our philosophy of leadership because they didn't; some thought that it was too egalitarian. But there were no clubhouse lawyers. If they fought the program, they didn't make it.

I looked for leaders who were hard-working, energetic, willing to take risks and be decisive. We forgave errors of commission but not errors of omission. I wanted managers who were fair and equitable, who didn't blame others but took on the responsibility themselves. Popularity, being elected to be in charge, can be very confusing. It's good for your confidence, and leaders must have confidence. But until people in charge understand that leadership isn't a popularity contest, they aren't leaders.

When people came to me with a problem I'd say, "What do you think we should do about it?" It's very hard to bluff your way out of that. Today, we have a lot of problems in the financial service industry, and the leadership that will succeed will be the leadership that can rally their people to the task of digging out of that trouble. It's not a question of are they in trouble. So decisiveness is important, and the leader's job is to chart the course to encourage the followership that will solve these very serious problems. Now, this is something that I refer to often when I'm speaking about leadership. In Matthew 4:19, Jesus said to the fishermen, Peter and Andrew, "Follow Me and I will make you fishers of men." What Jesus was offering was everlasting life. Now, flash forward to 1918 France, World War I and the Battle of Belleau Wood. Sergeant Dan Daly and a bunch of marines were pinned down in a wheat field under heavy fire from machine guns. These marines were getting slaughtered. Daly stood and shouted, "Come on, you sons of bitches. Do you want to live forever? Follow me!" And they did, they attacked the Germans with nothing but their bayonets and routed them. Now, my point is this: one man, Jesus, offered everlasting life. The other, Daly, offered almost sure death. Why did people follow them both? Well, people follow a leader because they believe that leader can take them somewhere that they can't go by themselves. And that's what leadership is really all about . . . followership.

Dr. Johnnetta B. Cole

To Whom Much Has Been Given, Much Is Required

Serves as chair of the Johnnetta B. Cole Global Diversity & Inclusion Institute founded at Bennett College for Women; president emerita, Spelman College and Bennett College for Women; taught at the University of California—Los Angeles, Washington State University—Pullman, the University of Massachusetts—Amherst, Hunter College, and Emory University

Telling each other our stories allows us to learn from and to connect with each other. There is power and I would say a kind of magic in sharing our stories, in recounting where we have been, and in dreaming about where we are going.

There is much about the story of my early life that is centered around strong leaders. Indeed, as I grew up, there were leaders who were pivotal in my life: my mother, Mary Frances Lewis Betsch, was clearly a leader, and to this day I am influenced by her strong belief in the power of education. As a youngster I greatly admired Dr. Mary McLeod Bethune, the great educator who counseled us all to lift others as we climb. And it is with great respect and fondness that I remember Professor George Eaton Simpson at Oberlin College, for it was his class in anthropology that changed the direction of my life from pursuing a career in medicine to studying anthropology.

My great-grandfather, Abraham Lincoln Lewis, was by any measure a great leader. A. L. Lewis, as everyone called him, was only one generation from slavery, he had only had an elementary school education, and he worked in a sawmill and then in a shoe store. But he went on to become the first black millionaire in Jacksonville, Florida.

My great-grandfather told me the story of how in 1901, he and six other African American men met to figure out how they could start a business that would help families who had a crisis such as the death of a bread winner or a serious illness that required expensive medical treatment. They came up with the idea that if each family put in a little money each week, when one of the families had a crisis then that family could receive a sizeable sum of money. This was the beginning of the Afro-American Life Insurance Company—the first insurance company in the state of Florida. When I became a student of anthropology, I learned that what those seven men had created was a version of a practice in West African societies called the SuSu.

A. L. Lewis was a deeply spiritual man who believed that at the core of leadership is the responsibility to serve others. He often referred to that passage in the Bible that says that from those to whom much has been given, much is required.

My great-grandfather died when I was eleven years old. But during those years that I did know him, he had a great influence on me. Every Sunday after church, my sister and I would go to his very stately home for dinner. I remember that he loved to tell my sister that there are three great books, and we should al-

ways make sure we had those three books in our lives, and understood the importance of each. The school book, my great-grandfather said, was the call for my own education. The bank book would help me gain financial security. And the Bible should be the center of my spiritual life. I didn't know it at that time, but A. L. Lewis was explaining to me some of his fundamental values, and he was calling on me to live by the same. When I think about who I am and what I have accomplished, I must acknowledge the influence of my great-grandfather. But I also acknowledge my parents, who taught by example rather than by platitudes.

I look at leadership not in terms of individuals who have enormous stature, visibility, or resources, but in terms of those who are capable of positively influencing others. A leader who clearly had a strong influence on me early in my life was Ms. Bunny Vance, my first-grade teacher. In those days of legal segregation, there were white schools and colored schools, and I of course went to a colored school. On the first day of class, Ms. Vance taught me an important lesson about leadership. It may be hard to believe, but I was a shy girl. When it was my turn to respond to Ms. Vance's instructions that each girl and boy should stand up and give their name, I had my head bowed and mumbled my name. Ms. Vance came to where I was standing and this is what she said: "Johnnetta, stand up straight, hold your head up, look directly at me and proudly say your name. That is what leaders do, and in this class, each of you will learn how to be a leader."

Governor James B. Hunt, Jr.

A Smart Start for Education

Four-term Democratic North Carolina governor; nationally recognized leader in education, an early proponent of teaching standards and early childhood education

During my life, I came to realize that one of the best ways to exercise leadership is to do it with partners. This leadership by partnership requires a lot of people working together to achieve success. Now, good leaders have to have good ideas, a vision. They have to understand the importance of ideas and that their own idea may need a lot more, a lot of vetting.

When we started Smart Start, a program that has been praised as one of the most innovative early childhood education programs in America, I had looked at what was going on in education in North Carolina and concluded that something was wrong, something was missing. We were putting a lot of money in education, but we weren't getting the big change that we needed. In studying that issue, I read a lot about early childhood education, learned about brain development of infants, discovered that children are born with about an equal number of brain cells, in the billions. But the potential for intelligence actually comes about when those little brain cells are connected. That's when a child becomes capable of learning, of having intelligence, the connecting up of those brain cells. So the importance of those early developmental years became clear.

Then I had an experience that really shaped me. I think that all good leaders can cite something that happened in their life that really touched them, that grabbed their attention. I used to run on my farm in Wilson County and on my route—across the interstate high-way—was an old ramshackle house. There were beer bottles covering the front yard, old worn-out cars up on blocks, and I noticed that this little child would come out the front door with a milk bottle in his hand trying to get some milk from the bottle. He'd be sucking this empty bottle, always in a diaper and nothing else, even during the coldest winter days. It was clear to me that there was nobody in that house taking care of that child. So I said to myself, "What chance is that child going to have? This isn't right!"

That gave me the moral courage to pursue something that I later learned that some other people were opposed to, providing early education for all the state's children. A good leader must have a sense of right and wrong. I knew it was wrong for that child to be so limited. I knew that child deserved a good start.

Later—this was 1992—while campaigning for my third term as governor, I was having dinner at a friend's house in Lenoir, North Carolina. The mother of that family was a kindergarten teacher, and we were talking about the status of children. She said, "Governor Hunt, I have children in my class who don't know their colors and don't even know their last names."

I couldn't imagine that, children in kindergarten who didn't know their colors, didn't know their last names? That helped confirm my thinking on this issue. So I took this early education of children to the people, made it a statewide conversation, made the link with the status of the children's early education and the schools' failures. If we were going to have our children be successful in school and expect them to get good jobs, then they were going to have to get a good start. Later we named it Smart Start—an excellent name, a great program.

But it was the partnership that made it work. And I listened to people. A good leader must read, talk, listen, have a conversation with people. It's their dollars, their community, their county, their state. So during that campaign in '92 I went to the people and said, "Let's make a decision here about what we're going to do about our schools, about education." I laid out my idea: to give these children a good start, to provide high-quality early childhood education for them and to help their parents be successful. Again, this was in my campaign for the governorship in 1992: there were town hall gatherings, one-on-one conversations. The people of North Carolina answered by re-electing me overwhelmingly for a third term, and in doing so, they were saying what they wanted to do about one of the biggest problems in the state. They didn't just elect a governor; they made a commitment to education for young children, to Smart Start.

Now, getting the funding through the state legislature wasn't easy. But I never gave up, worked day and night, and did it with the help and the partnership of the local communities—schools, libraries, churches, businesses, local governments. We developed a nonprofit corporation at the state level called the North Carolina Partnership for Children and a nonprofit corporation in each county. Some folks were opposed. But all we wanted to do was to make sure that every child had a good childhood center to go to, good teachers, good facilities, and a safe place to play.

Smart Start, the North Carolina Partnership for Children, is about helping our children become the best they can be, all that they can be, should be and must be: all that God would want them to be. Today, it's a successful program, nationally recognized. The key or secret to that success was this: the leadership was a partnership, a partnership with the caring people of North Carolina.

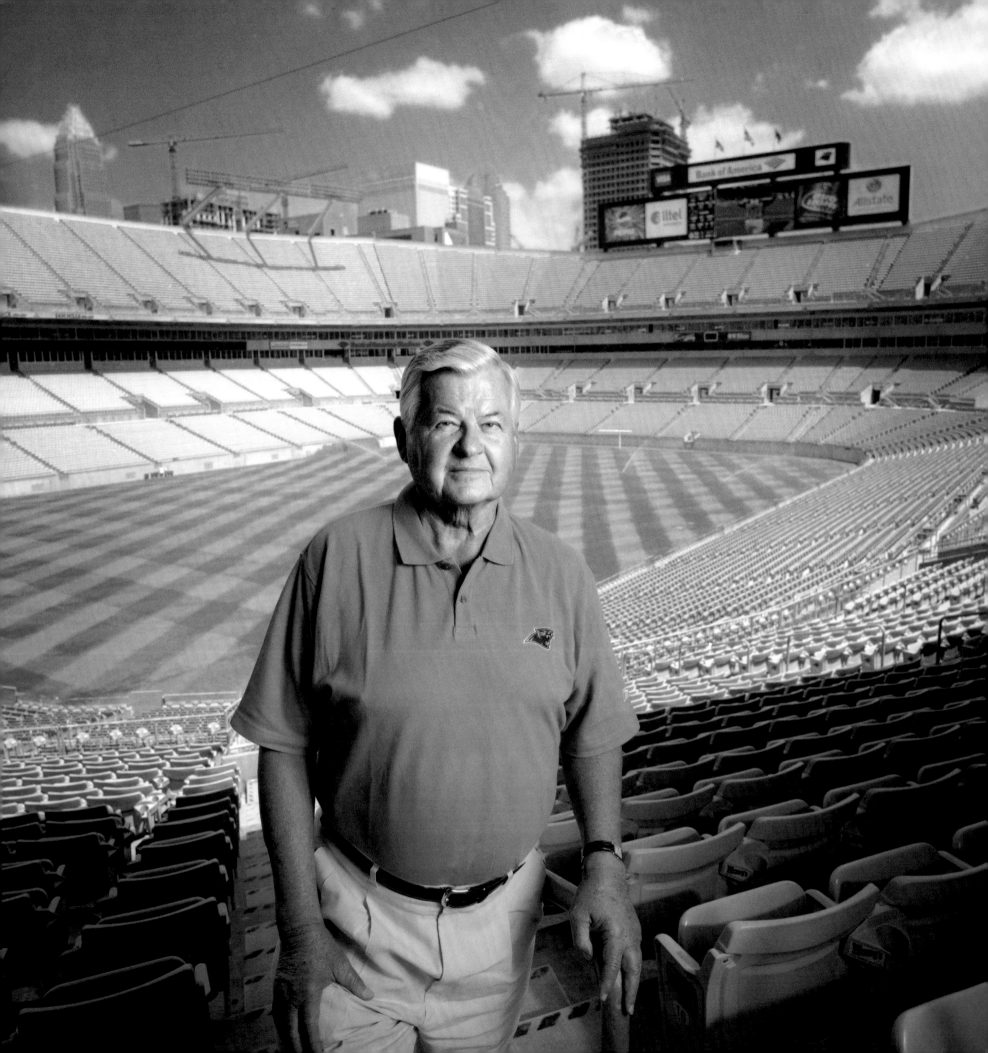

Jerry Richardson

Bringing the NFL to the Carolinas

Realized a career-long goal when his investment team was awarded the twenty-ninth franchise of the NFL, the Carolina Panthers; CEO of TW Services, which became Flagstar, the largest publicly held company based in South Carolina, with interests in more than 2,500 restaurants (among other holdings) and more than 100,000 employees

How NFL football came to the Carolinas is a story about leadership, partnership, and something that may surprise some people. It's about a culture, the culture where I was raised in eastern North Carolina. Where I grew up, basic principles like modesty, good manners, and integrity made a difference. If you told someone that you were going to do something, they expected you to do it. It was a badge of honor, a huge disappointment if you couldn't come through. Now our goal wasn't to try to get NFL football for Charlotte, honestly it really wasn't. The goal was to bring NFL football to the Carolinas. I'd seen the impact that an NFL franchise can have on the emotions of a city like Baltimore, which was where I played. Those people lived each week looking forward to Sunday. We wanted that for the Carolinas. The competition for this franchise here was tough, a lot of great cities and a lot of influence. We were competing with places like Baltimore, St. Louis, Jacksonville, San Antonio, Oakland, and Memphis, and we were the biggest long shot of all.

How did all this happen? I think a lot of this goes back to that culture I was talking about. I was fifty years old when we started the process to bring this team here, and for the first time in my life, I had no debt on our home. If you owned your home where I grew up that was a big thing; it's not a big deal anymore, but it was a big deal then. This was January 1987 and I wrote to Hugh McColl and told him about this idea and that, for the first time in my life, I had no debt. I operated a large business and he'd been loaning me money for a long time. By April we were on our way, trying to get this franchise. Things changed in a hurry. I was right back in my old rut, borrowing money, trying to convince people of influence that this was a good idea. One of the things that helped us had to do with those people with whom we were associating. These people were giving me time and support—this fed off of itself, gave others confidence. The fact that we were going to fund our own stadium, not rely on the taxpayers, made it a tougher sell to the NFL.

We were going to borrow a lot of money. So the banks were the key. Wachovia, First Union, and Bank of America—which used to be NationsBank—were all major competitors, and these banks didn't have a history of doing things together. There was a lot of hard work, a lot of negotiating, and frankly, a lot of unknowns. Eventually this all ended up in the office of Bill Lee, the CEO of Duke Power, a great man. This was in June of 1993, and we went into that room knowing that when we came out a decision had to have been made. We couldn't be wishy-washy, we had to make a commitment to each other.

All of us had to make a decision that day—Hugh McColl, NationsBank; John Medlin, Wachovia; Ed Crutchfield, First Union; Roger Milliken, the Milliken Company; and Bill Lee. We had to say this is going to work, and we are going to get it done. We couldn't even talk about what would happen if we didn't do it. Now, you talk about commitment. We left that room knowing that every time we wrote a check, if we didn't get this franchise, the money was gone.

There were numerous other partners who came aboard, all with great influence and reputations, all committed to bringing the NFL to the Carolinas. As I look back on all this, there were some basic keys to this success, keys that we've used in all our business endeavors. If you're going to be successful, someone is going to have to work hard. Secondly, you must have harmony. The third thing is teamwork. The fourth key is to listen; you must be aware. Finally, there's respect. All this goes back to that eastern North Carolina culture—hard work, harmony, teamwork, listen or be aware, and be respectful. Later, after we'd been awarded the franchise in 1993, Pete Rozelle, who was then the NFL's commissioner, said, "This NFL franchise will change the Carolinas forever. It's like nothing that's ever happened there." And he was right. It's a slow process, generational, one that will get there sooner depending on how well we perform. But it would be hard for most people to comprehend what it means to us to walk into this beautiful stadium recalling the leadership that brought it here and knowing how much a franchise like this one cares about its team, its fans, and the people of the Carolinas.

Dr. Catherine Gordon

Making Inroads in Medicine

Co-founder and director of the Bone Health Program at Children's Hospital Boston and associate professor of pediatrics, Harvard Medical School; carrying out research in anorexia nervosa, vitamin D and pediatric bone health, and cystic fibrosis–related bone disease

I always loved science. When I was twelve years old, I was a candy striper at Rex Hospital in Raleigh and met a pediatrician, Dr. Marjorie Carr, who became a role model and mentor for me. So I started thinking about pediatrics when I was thirteen. Premed in NC State's College of Agriculture and Life Sciences was a good fit for me, and when I was in medical school at UNC, I was considering adult medicine and pediatric surgery. But in the end, pediatrics was my choice and I've never regretted it. There's such an opportunity to be a role model and to work with children and their families.

When I was in my residency at Children's Hospital, I started thinking about how hormones affect the skeleton, how growth hormones, the pubertal hormones—testosterone and estrogen—make the bones stronger. And, when they're not in evidence, why the bones would be weaker. An adult endocrinologist, Dr. Meryl Leboff, took me under her wing and said, "There really isn't a person in pediatric medicine who thinks about the skeleton. You should take this on."

Now that I head the Bone Health Program at Children's Hospital, I'm often asked why a pediatrician would be interested in osteoporosis, because it's thought to be a disease of the elderly and not typically found in children. Well, about a decade ago, we realized that there were children who had washed-out X-rays, kids with frequent fractures, and all we had were adult standards to use in determining whether it was osteoporosis or not. So I took this on as a personal mission. We opened the Bone Center in 2000 and have had great success here. But this wasn't accomplished without the help of some incredible mentors like Dr. Leboff, people whose leadership allowed me to teach, pursue nontraditional research, and, as a result, make some inroads in this area of medicine.

For over a decade now, we've been taking care of patients and have had a research component where anyone at the hospital who's interested in bone disease in children can come for information.

Most of the children I care for range from school age to young adults. Examples of these diseases would be Crohn's disease, rickets, cystic fibrosis, and anorexia nervosa. In girls with anorexia nervosa, we've been looking for a cure for the bone loss associated with this disease. The National Institutes of Health thought this work was important, so I was fortunate enough to win the Presidential Early Career Award for Scientists and Engineers. I appreciate the leadership from the people who develop and present awards like this because they are more than just recognition. They bring awareness to important research and programs.

An example of this is our work with vitamin D deficiency. I'd been picking up all this vitamin D deficiency in my bone clinic in at-risk children, so I launched a large study in our healthy adolescent clinic. When healthy adolescents came in for check-ups, we ran vitamin D tests and found that 42 percent were vita-min D–deficient. These were huge, very surprising numbers. Not only children with bone disease and fractures but healthy kids were deficient. That research has set off multiple studies, with scientists looking at different disease groups for vitamin D deficiency—and not just at Children's Hospital but across the country. We've learned that most of us, all age groups, are vitamin D–deficient.

I knew that this had important public health implications and presented these findings at the national meeting of the Endocrine Society in Philadelphia. The media picked up on this and, pretty soon, I was being interviewed by newspapers and on national TV. I'm a naturally shy person, but I realized that sometimes what might appear to be self-serving to someone in a leadership position isn't, that there are times when you have to get the word out and that it's for the greater good. People needed to know that we're living in a society where kids play indoors more, aren't getting sufficient sunlight, and don't drink the fortified milk they need. The result has been a national awareness about vitamin D deficiency and collaboration from other doctors, leaders in this field, people who are helping us move this effort in the right direction.

Over the years I've realized what an important role leadership plays in my work. I was blessed by some wonderful mentors and, for young scientists, a mentor is so important. So part of my mission is to coach young scientists the way I've been coached, taking the time to give them both positive and negative feedback. As academic doctors, we are so busy in the hospital; there's always a sick patient, a class to teach, a grant due. There's no room for error with patients, so it's easy to forget to take the time to give your team positive feedback. But I try to remember to mix the positive feedback with the negative, that good leaders will always take the time to discuss what's going well and why.

Governor James E. Holshouser, Jr.

The Right Place at the Right Time

Governor of North Carolina, 1973–1977; strong supporter of consolidation of The University of North Carolina under a Board of Governors

Sometimes leadership is like starting the car on a cold morning and hoping the engine will turn over. There were a number of leadership initiatives during my years of public service where I just helped to get things started—programs that achieved meaningful results. Some people wake up in the morning with ten new ideas (with perhaps eight needing to go in the trash can but still leaving you with two good ones). I've never considered myself to be one of those people but have believed in that old maxim, "The harder you work, the luckier you get." If you don't worry about who gets the credit, you can get a lot of things done. Sometimes it's timing and luck involved, but if you have good people around you, if you read, listen, and sift through what others are saying, you can pick and choose the right ideas and projects, then put your oar in the water and make a contribution.

I do believe that leaders in government need to understand about the money—where it comes from, what events can affect the flow of it into the state treasury, and how different sources of funds affect how to spend it. During my governorship our first executive order established an Efficiency Study Commission, which made recommendations that saved the taxpayers over eighty million dollars every year. Good money management let us double the state's park land and give community colleges their first capital money since they got started. There were other examples of what people might call success, but I think it is important to note that almost all required leadership from a lot of people—not just me. When I was in the legislature, Governor Scott began an important pilot program for kindergartens. Then C. D. Spangler and W. T. Harris persuaded me that we should take the effort statewide, and they were key leaders in that initiative. We expanded AHEC (area health education centers) and created a network of rural health centers to try to improve the health care in our rural areas. I cared a lot about both of those, but Dr. Jim Bernstein was the genius who really did the heavy lifting and made North Carolina a rural health-care model for the country. We were able to create a legislative coalition to pass the Coastal Area Management Act and a number of other environmental issues. There may be no better example of coalition building than the effort to save the New River, a leadership effort where Republicans and Democrats, North Carolinians from all walks of life, joined forces to prevent the flooding of farm lands in Ashe and Alleghany Counties and "keep the New River as it is."

As I look back, my involvement with the restructuring of public higher education may have been my most important contribution to North Carolina. In the legislature, I'd watched battles being fought among our campuses, with each one having its own agendas, lobbyists, and coalitions. Higher education was being poorly served, and taxpayer dollars weren't getting the most bang for the buck. Governor Scott appointed a study commission led by Senator Lindsay Warren—a good choice, since Lindsay is smart and well respected. The study commission report suggested that we consolidate all of the campuses under a coordinated board. I thought it was a good report but that we needed a strong governing board, rather than one that just coordinated. I had heard that the Georgia system might be worth some study. So I drove down and talked to Governor Jimmy Carter and then went over to see Cotton Robinson, who'd grown up in western North Carolina and was the number two man at the Georgia Board of Regents. Cotton agreed to come to North Carolina, and I took him to see Governor Scott and key legislators in the House and Senate. Slowly but surely, the train moved onto the right track. Leaders need to be persuasive, and it was Cotton who made the case for this governing body that would eventually become the University of North Carolina Board of Governors. It was frankly a political miracle that we were able to pull enough people together to create the new, multi-campus University of North Carolina. In many ways, the university has set North Carolina apart and above the rest of the South—in fact, above most states in the nation. I just sort of helped start that engine, and in the end, it became an educational system that will help North Carolina and the nation face the economic challenges of the twenty-first century.

Franklin Graham

Keeping the Faith

Christian evangelist; president and CEO of the international Christian relief organization Samaritan's Purse, which responds to the wars, diseases, and disasters of the world, and the Billy Graham Evangelistic Association

To be a leader you have to set the example. You can't ask someone to do something unless you are willing to do it yourself. In the early days, Samaritan's Purse was small, only me and a secretary. So we did everything. As more people came in, we still shared the load. And even today (more than five hundred employees), when there is a heavy snow day and the parking lot gets full, we all take turns shoveling snow. I think that's part of being a leader; you set an example. But you have to set that example in your personal life as well; you have to have integrity, your word has to mean something. Having that type of trust, that type of bond, is a great part of leadership.

Over the years, I've heard some wonderful one-liners about leadership. But I find it to be something that you deal with every day. Just because you had a good day yesterday doesn't mean that you're going to have a good one today. And your word, well, that has to be the same.

The best example of leadership that I can think of is my father. He gave leadership to his ministry of over sixty years, a ministry that has worldwide impact and touched millions of lives around the world. My father was the same person at home as he was in public. There weren't two Billy Grahams. I remember when John Wayne died; of course, he was an actor and, to many of my generation, a hero. I remember one of his sons talking about the John Wayne that people saw on the silver screen being the same John Wayne that he saw at home. I thought about that, and I thought that's my father, the Billy Graham the world has seen in the big stadiums and on the television screen is the same we've seen at home. That's not always true of public figures; many times there's a game face, there is this public person, but when the cameras are off, it's a different person. You have to be the same person in private life as you are in public life.

Another important leadership lesson that I learned from my father was one of the integrity of finances. When my father came into his ministry, evangelists were not respected, they were viewed as charlatans: people who came in, had a big meeting, took up a love offering, and then left the community with buckets of money. My father was the first of the Christian leaders to say, "I'm going to form a board of directors and I'm going to have that board of directors set my salary. They will manage the business affairs of the organization, and I will manage the ministry. They won't tell me where or what to preach; I'll take that from the Lord. But I want these people around me to make sure the business has that integrity."

Of course, leadership isn't just one thing; it's so many different things. Good leaders learn from people, watch those who have been successful, and then sometimes just say, "I'm going to copy that, do it exactly the way they did it because it worked."

Samaritan's Purse exists for the purpose of taking the wars, the diseases, the disasters of this world and helping people in their hour of need. But as a Christian leader, I want to do this in the name of God's Son, Jesus Christ. So at Samaritan's Purse, we help people and we do it in the name of Christ. When Jesus was here on earth, hungry people came to Him, He fed them. When the sick came to Him, He healed them. Even the dead in His presence were raised to life. Jesus never turned His back on any person who came to Him in need. I just think if Jesus Christ were on earth today, then this would be the question: would He be in the middle of the AIDS epidemic in Africa? Yes, He would. If He were here today, would He be down on the Gulf Coast helping those people who lost all their homes after Hurricane Ike? Absolutely. When Hurricane Katrina hit New Orleans, would you have found Jesus Christ in the flooded Ninth Ward helping to rescue? Yes, you would. I want every person that we help to know there is a God who loves them and cares for them, a God who has provided a way for them to be with Him in heaven and that's to have faith in His Son, Jesus Christ.

Leadership is something that God gives you. He gives you the insight and instincts to do the right thing. Leaders have to make those right decisions, not do what's most expedient or best for the moment, but do what is the best for the ministry, the business, the nation, and the world.

Rear Admiral Ralph E. Suggs, USN (R)

Captain of His Ship

Carrier commanding officer and retired rear admiral, United States Navy, and Harley-Davidson senior executive

Leadership is about relationships. I don't care if you're the captain of the carrier USS *America* or a Harley-Davidson executive. It's about being able to articulate and communicate a vision that's shared. Everyone has to understand the leader's vision, and then it becomes about overachieving. I grew up in the sticks of North Carolina on a dirt road down in Columbus County. Other than my parents, my mother particularly, the person who influenced me the most was my granddaddy. When his health deteriorated, I had the opportunity to run his farm. He respected people and I'll never forget this. He told me, "Don't ever abuse employees. Without them, we wouldn't have an opportunity to provide a living for ourselves or for them." I've never forgotten that, and it was that, his integrity and overachieving, that influenced me. Later as the captain of the aircraft carrier USS *America*, I had an opportunity to call up some of those core values. I was very lucky; I had my choice of captaining three great carriers—the *John F. Kennedy*, the *Kitty Hawk*, and the *America*. I chose the *America* because she was in her last deployment and would be at sea the most, be in a position to be in harm's way. Plus, her call sign was COURAGE. That came with a lot of responsibility and was one hell of an honor, and I took it that way.

Very soon, I faced a career-defining leadership moment. Shortly after taking command, we had a major boiler explosion which did about five million dollars in damage. Once I found out my troops were okay and I'd looked at the damage, knowing that she was only scheduled to make one more deployment, I knew somebody was going to have to make a very tough decision, even though Bosnia and the Adriatic issues were out there and they really needed this warship. But were they going to spend that kind of money? Well, here's where the leadership comes in. A preliminary investigation had called it human error, slammed the crew. This proved to be unfounded, and then the JAG report came out, which absolved all of my crew from any wrongdoing; the boiler itself was an accident waiting to happen. So Vice Admiral "Sweet Pea" Dick Allen asked me a very basic question: "Can you do it, make this ship seaworthy?" And thanks to him, I had a very interesting leadership moment. I said, "Yes, hell yes," then Admiral Allen allowed me to stand in front of that crew, a group whose hearts were broken, sailors who'd been out to sea for months, and tell them they all had an option. They could accept their fitness reports, which would go up to the day before the mishap, and leave the *America*. Those who left would go to onshore duty. Then I said, "If you decide to stay to make this ship battle worthy, well, like my granddaddy used to say, 'You better be prepared to get your asses off the porch and run with the big dogs!'" Then I gave them a weekend leave to think it over. On the following Monday morning there wasn't a single sailor who left that ship. Now, we worked our tails off, overachieved, painted the ship ourselves, and this baby's 1,100 feet long, has 110,000 parts. When we finally brought her out to sea, she looked like a brand-new '55 Chevy.

Some very proud, overachieving sailors were on board. In a very short time the *America* was selected by General Schoomaker over several other carriers to take his special operations troops into Haiti. Again, vision, commitment, and overachievers. We were selected because we were willing to take the *America* closer to the proposed target, a bit risky in a claw-like coral bay harbor just off Haiti, but we weighed the risks against rewards, and the rewards were substantial. We were going to save seven to eight minutes in helicopter flights from the carrier to the mission. And, as General Schoomaker said, "That could be the difference in life and death to one of my Rangers." That was a successful mission, and later not only did *America* win the Battle Efficiency Award, which is the best carrier out of six carriers on the East Coast, she got the Battenberg Cup, which is given to the best ship in the Atlantic fleet. Now, if it hadn't been for that "big dog" approach, the vision for this ship, and the leadership and trust and commitment of men like Admiral Allen and General Schoomaker, none of this would have been possible. They put everything professionally and personally on the line because they believed in a few thousand men and their crazy skipper. I believe there are some basic points to leadership—vision, passion, determination, a sense of humor. But there's one more, the most important. It's your heart. The heart is the X factor of leadership.

Herman Boone

Remembering the Titans

Head football coach, T. C. Williams High School, Alexandria, Virginia, and subject of the film Remember the Titans, *portrayed by Denzel Washington; played a key role in the integration of a school system in northern Virginia*

During the late '60s and early '70s, people in the United States were looking for leadership. It was a time when America was under great stress, dealing with the Vietnam War, *The Pentagon Papers*, Black Panthers, civil rights, the integration of schools. All these things came together, and people were just sort of waking up angry. With the demonstrations during those times and the disdain for law, leadership was badly needed. I believe that leaders are willing to sacrifice their personal gains to show people the light on the other side of the tunnel; that's what I tried to do coaching the Titans at T. C. Williams High School in Alexandria, Virginia.

If you saw the movie *Remember the Titans* with Denzel Washington playing my part, you'll recall that there were two young men on that championship team at T. C. Williams, Julius Campbell and Gary Bertier: one black, the other white. With the integration at T. C. Williams, they were tossed into this pool of hate, a dislike for each other based on the colors of their skins. It took the leadership of Coach Yoast (the white head coach who was passed over for the integrated school's head coaching job and stayed on as assistant) and me to show them that people are not judged on the colors of their skins but as individuals. Campbell and Bertier became significant leaders on that integrated championship team, and in doing so, helped take a school system and school that had been fighting integration forward, forward in a very positive way.

When I left North Carolina in 1969, I didn't leave because I wanted to. I'd won five championships in Williamston, but the superintendent of schools told me that the town of Williamston, which was integrating, wasn't ready for a black head coach.

So I went off to northern Virginia to coach, signed that contract not knowing that I was jumping out of the frying pan into the fire. I went there as an assistant coach for a lot more money than I was making in North Carolina. Then, the next year, they consolidated three high schools into one—T. C. Williams. I was chosen, without my knowledge or my permission, to be the head coach of that integrated school and chosen over a legendary coach, Yoast, a white man who had an incredible record and following. There was some of the hatred that comes with prejudice and unwanted change, but we made it work. I used to tell Coach Yoast that people say, "Coach Boone, you and Coach Yoast put your differences aside." And I'd say, "What differences? The only difference between the two of us is the pigmentation of our skin." We never saw color or race as a detriment. And together, we provided the leadership that made that integrated team work and win.

Now this wasn't without its leadership challenges. But I was up to that challenge, and I think the reason goes right back to leaders like Dr. Martin Luther King. I didn't march with Dr. King, but I was one of the few teachers in North Carolina who joined him, worked with his appointed persons in that civil rights movement in eastern North Carolina. Sarah Smalls, Golden Frinks, Mary Mobley, and Cleo Lee were all great leaders, people who stood up even in the face of losing their jobs. This was a time when a number of us said, "Enough is enough." I was not going to raise my child to believe that she wasn't worthy, so we stood up, and I did a lot of things that probably irritated a lot of people, but I was fighting for my rights to be a human being.

Another leader who prepared me for that challenge at T. C. Williams was my father, Frank Boone. He couldn't read or write, but he was a brilliant man, the man who taught me about leadership, about opportunities and optimism. He used to say, "Children, there's nothing you can do about the break of day. It will come whether you like it or not. If you don't plan to make a difference during that day then you can take yourself back to sleep." So many black people back then, and for a good reason, thought that the light at the other end of the tunnel was a train coming right at them. My father always had a smile for everyone, and he led our family, led us kids to believe that it wasn't necessarily the headlights of a train coming our way, but opportunity. Now, when I think about leadership, I remember what General MacArthur said, "There is no security anywhere on this earth, only opportunity." And, that's what leaders do . . . seize opportunities.

Alan Dickson

Operating by the Honor Code

Consolidated the R.S. Dickson Company with American & Efird Mills, one of the world's leading manufacturers and distributors of sewing thread for industrial and consumer markets, while co-founding the Ruddick Corporation with his brother, Stuart Dickson, establishing one of North Carolina's leading firms as a diversified holding company with components that include investment banking, sewing threads, computers, business forms, golf carts, and the Harris Teeter chain of grocery stores

I was blessed by being associated with some excellent leaders. In the 1940s, I went away to McCallie School in Chattanooga, Tennessee. It was a college preparatory school and where I needed to be. I wasn't a bad kid, incorrigible maybe. It was a military school at the time, and I entered McCallie as a private and graduated as a private. I guess that tells you something about my nature. I wasn't defiant, just always into mischief. They had a system there where they recorded your grades, and this covered behavior as well, and you ended up in a class—A, B, C, D, and E. E was the bottom. My academics were pretty good, deportment not so good. I ended up in E class.

My senior English teacher, Bill Pressley, was an outstanding secondary educator and later became the founding headmaster of Westminster School in Atlanta. When you talk about leaders, he was not a man of tall stature, but very precise and epitomized perfection. Of course, I'll never forget Major Burns. He headed up the boarding program—a soft heart, but a tough way. Always saw to it that we had plenty of milk and peanut butter on the dining room tables, and boy, if you acted up in that dining hall of his, he'd just spin around, look at you and shout, "You. Out!" We're raising money right now at McCallie to build a dormitory in Major Burns' name.

They used the paddle at McCallie back then. Buck Flowers was the Spanish teacher, the football and tennis coach. And Buck always said, "You can't learn a foreign language if you don't know your vocabulary. And, if you make below eighty on my vocabulary quizzes, you're going to get this paddle." Like I said, he was the tennis coach, and he had an unbelievable forehand.

All of these men, in their own way, were great teachers and leaders.

Dr. McCallie was the headmaster. He was another one of those manifestations of authority, a very religious guy, values-oriented, strong on character. Well, one night there was a bit of mischief, a trick we played on one of the professors in a study hall. Now, we're all on the honor code, and Dr. McCallie asked us, "Who are the perpetrators of this?"

Well, one by one, our hands go up. They just automatically went up; you just didn't question it . . . that was the McCallie way. He took us to his office and gave us a choice. We could take the punishment—a paddling—and remain in E class (detention) the rest of the year, or be put on a bus that night and sent home. I chose E class and the paddling. Dr. McCallie was no Buck Flowers, but he could hit.

I look back at that night and remember leadership. We were called on to own up, to admit our transgressions, stand and take our medicine.

That leadership stuck, because later in business when we formed the Ruddick Corporation, we bought an apparel company that belonged to Monsanto. Early on, we were able to capture revenue from the cash flow, and that enabled us to pay for the business. And so, we're pretty smart now, and we're going to grow this thing bigger. This was a classic mistake of your zeal getting in front of judgment. This was a New York company and there was a very difficult labor union. The customer list was tough, retailers in New York were tough, and if something didn't sell, they'd just return it to you alleging quality issues. Long story short, this company of ours got in trouble, and we had to report this to our directors.

And we were kind of like deer in the headlights—quite frankly, a young management team. Well, typically in this industry, people just bankrupted these businesses. If they'd run into a problem with a company, they'd bankrupt it. So I stood up with my report, and I told our directors that we always had that choice. Addison Reese was the chairman of the old NCNB Corporation, and he was on our board. And if there was anyone who I looked up to—other than my father—it was Addison Reese. He was a quiet man, not an out-front man, but had exceptional leadership skills. He ran a tight ship and was a great mentor and teacher. He said, "Alan, you know better than that! We're here in North Carolina, and you're operating by the mores of this part of the world. You operate this business the way you were raised and how you were taught. Don't even think about bankrupting that company."

Not only was he dead right, it made me feel so bad to have offered that option. Because I was raised to do the right thing, and certainly if you go back to those folks that I mentioned at McCallie—Major Burns, Buck Flowers, Bill Pressley, and Dr. McCallie—well, they all taught us the same values that I'd learned at home, taught us all to do the right thing.

Dr. Carmaleta Littlejohn Monteith

Leadership by Example

Educational consultant; president, North American Indian Women's Association; Cherokee cultural preservationist

My mother was a single parent, clearly a leader. Although she was married, my father always worked away. He'd been trained to be a linotype operator and a painter, and so his work was in the cities. He sent money home to us but I have to attribute my upbringing to the influence of my mother. When we were growing up, there weren't many resources in the tribe here on the reservation. Leadership was taught by example. We learned by watching and by doing. We had to live off the land. The Cherokee Boys Club is an example of a leadership initiative that was very, very successful. They established the farming program where the boys worked outside in the fields, and I remember as a little girl that we were always taught to do something, either working in the kitchen or with crafts.

I grew up as the eldest sibling and so I was always helping my mother. And she did so many things. She had a shop in downtown Cherokee where we sold local handcrafts. We lived there in the back of the shop. This was before Sears Roebuck started marketing this product, but I remember her having huge spools of chenille thread which she used to make bedspreads and housecoats. She loved to sew and, in fact, the one craft we all developed was bead working. She made beautiful beadwork, and during the long hard winters we all beaded. My father's family were basket weavers. The basket weaving was more involved; you had to go to the woods and cut down the trees, and it took a long time to prepare for basket weaving. Because my mother's beadwork was of such high quality, we never had any trouble selling it. I'll never forget that my mother ran an ad in *Boy's Life* Magazine called Chief Drowning Bear; we were descendants of this great chief. Well, we made and sold rock tomahawks, bows and arrows, dance bells, and whips. The whips were very popular but difficult to make. You had to braid four strands, and the braiding was normally three strands, but we learned to do it and then we shipped them out. So that was part of our industry.

In those early years—this was the 1940s—the only way we had to earn a living was through these crafts. You didn't take classes; the skills were just passed down through the families. Then you would be recognized for who you were by your craft. You'd be a potter or basket weaver, a beader.

In the old days, we had an economy of exchange in bartering, and in our tribe something called Gadugi, which is Cherokee for free labor or free hand. And it exists today in some of our communities, where people will help each other with no charge—build houses, dig graves, work gardens. In the earlier years, my mother started a food co-op, and I thought this was so funny because she would rent these huge trucks, climb up in the cab, and off she'd go to buy cases of groceries wholesale and then bring them back to the community. She trained a lot of people here, taught them that they could mark up the goods 7 percent and make a profit.

So my mother was clearly a leader, but the greatest gift she gave me was her understanding of the need for and the importance of education. She always read to us and gave us her appreciation of books. Now, I'll admit that I always had a passion for teaching. When I was a little girl, when we'd play pretend I always wanted to be the teacher. But my mother and father made sure that I went to public school where I could learn math, science, take a foreign language. And it was there that I was influenced by other leaders. I remember Gertrude Flanagan in the old Cherokee boarding school that we went to here on the reservation. She's the one who encouraged my parents to send me off to public school in Bryson City. I had a homeroom teacher there named John Wikle. Now, here was a man who on our homeroom time read to us, and he was the one who set me on the right path, helped me with my resumé, and made sure that I went off to college!

I've had a long career in education, math, and the sciences. It was at the Lovett School and the Marist School in Atlanta where my own leadership skills surfaced as an administrator. And over the years, I, along with a number of my colleagues, have served associations that I hope have done some good: the Eastern Band of Cherokee Indians, the Cherokee Indian Hospital, Cherokee Youth Center Advisory Committee, and the Yogi Crowe Scholarship Fund Advisory Board, which was started by my mother, along with others, to honor a young Cherokee man who lost his life in a car accident.

More than anything else, leadership is about one word and that's commitment. You can't just sign on. You have to commit. When people tell me they don't know how I do so much, I have a unique perspective on this: I look back at my mother and other leaders and what they managed to accomplish. There are times today when I have to say no, only because I know I can't commit. But when I'm asked to contribute my time to anything to do with Indian affairs, I think back to my mother, my upbringing, and my Cherokee heritage—and can't help but commit.

Charlie Rose

Listening for Leadership

Host of the PBS show Charlie Rose, *has conducted more than 100,000 interviews, many with some of the great leaders of the world—Nelson Mandela, Salman Rushdie, Bill Gates, Jimmy Carter, Bill Clinton, George H. W. Bush, and George W. Bush*

The desire to be a leader is important. But you have to have done something circumstantially in a life or in a competition that merits others saying, "I know where they are coming from and I believe in their authenticity." Leadership isn't about marketing, salesmanship, or just because you can make a speech. The essence of a leader comes from many things, the content of a life, from experience, from the capacity to communicate the mission—be it military, science, business, sports, or the arts. Leaders have to be able to lay out a plan to achieve victory. People who will be followed believe in themselves and are able to articulate what everybody's responsibility is and how this is all knit together as a part of the total mission. Those who follow must believe in that leader, and in the end, the result can be teamwork.

The thing that's missing from leadership, at least from my observation, is being able to define that mission and to convince a number of people to believe in it. This goes back to that key to leadership, the ability to communicate, to resonate the responsibilities of the team and how they will be held accountable. Too often I find that people don't know what is expected of them. It's important that those who would follow know how tough it's going to be and why the leader believes in them, believes they are up to the challenge. This instills confidence. You must believe that your leader is prepared—that he or she will work hard, that they care more about the mission than you do and care equally about you. So great leaders are prepared—physically, intellectually, emotionally.

And that's where leadership begins.

I've seen a whole range of leaders come to the table (interviews on *Charlie Rose*), people who have shown courage and have a commitment to human life. A number of military people define this. But leadership doesn't come with a single act of courage or a single sacrifice. While admirable, those who have exhibited this type of heroics may not have been looking at the entire voyage or seeing the big picture. I believe most great military leaders think about their troops and do everything that they can for them. They also have the courage to shoulder the burden, to take all responsibilities for their command. General Eisenhower left a message going into Normandy and D-Day saying that if things went badly, in the end it was his fault. Then there's that X factor of leadership that some call charisma. There have been times when this charisma that I'm talking about comes from someone who may surprise you. Someone who looks rather ordinary on stage or at work is suddenly thrown into action and they become ennobled by the challenge. With a leader like Nelson Mandela, well, the charisma is obvious. But, as to leadership, if you consider what my recent guests said about Mandela (Richard Stengle, editor of *Time* Magazine and a Mandela biographer, and Margaret Marshall, the twenty-third chief justice of the Massachusetts Supreme Judicial Court, who led students who opposed South Africa's racist apartheid system) you will learn some very interesting lessons. When Mandela talked about fear from a leader's perspective, he said that courage is not the absence of fear. But as a leader he was able to mask it and then inspire others to go beyond it. I've never known anyone that I truly admired that wasn't really interested in the lives and the opinions of the people that they wanted to join them in a great endeavor, Mandela exemplified this belief. I also think that Mandela was right when he said that in order to lead one must know who the other person or other country is. In short it is important to know one's adversary, your competitor, to know the circumstance. To know them better and what to expect of them, he learned the Afrikaans language, their interests, their culture, and their passion for sports like rugby.

One of my concerns is that this awareness (that Mandela exhibited) and the idea of listening and leadership has lost some of its meaning. Executives in business need to listen, to understand their customers. A quarterback needs to listen to what that wide receiver tells him because the receiver has a different perspective of the cornerback from his position on the field. Everyone I know who has accomplished something has wanted to hear what others think. What you say matters to them. Most importantly, in terms of the United States and our leadership in our world affairs, we should want to know what others think. I believe that the world wants the United States to lead. But they also want to know that we are listening.

Dr. LeRoy Walker

Leadership through Followship

First African American selected head coach of the U.S. Olympic Track and Field Team, first African American president of the U.S. Olympic Committee, and former chancellor, North Carolina Central University

My father died when I was very young. The lady who got me off in the right direction was that wonderful woman I called Big Momma. There were eleven of us, a big family, and I was the youngest. So she watched over me, and then later when I was older, I teased her saying, "Big Momma, people don't know the impact that you had on me. You know, you could speak volumes with your eyes." I'd be messing around doing things, and she'd cut those eyes of hers at me, and I knew what that meant. So Big Momma was an influence. Later, she allowed me to go to New York to live with my brother Joe, the man who taught me more about leadership than any other.

But there were others. We lived only a block and a half from Morehouse College in Atlanta. There were coaches there, leaders who would have the greatest impact on my life as an athlete, be the influence that got me into coaching. They all took me into their arms. I became their mascot. I was, like, nine years old and what an adhesion that was; I mean the way I stuck to them. This was my first lesson in leadership. I felt the belief they had in me and was able to transfer that belief into a tremendous sense of personal confidence. This confidence helped me win all-state honors in track and had an impact later when I went off to Benedict College, where I played basketball, football, and ran track. The Bene-

dict coaches called me Po Belly (poor belly) because I had a little tummy that stuck out. But they knew I could run; they saw that I had a talent. One of my mentors there, Professor Dad Crawford, seemed to always have a stopwatch. I think this is why I became a sprinter. He wouldn't ask me to run the 220 or the 100. "Po Belly, run to the end of the gym, run to that building over there." And then he'd time me. These Benedict elders didn't tell me, they showed me what leadership meant. I lived it, experienced the reality of leadership. So I was blessed by this experience, and I think it's why I'm so dedicated now to something I call leadership/followship. I learned that you can't just talk about leading; you have to lead and then pay attention, make sure that someone is following.

Let me tell you about my brother Joe. He was a New York contractor in the window-cleaning business. I moved to New York and grew up in his house as a teenager, and he gave me a great idea of what leadership meant, something that I could mimic—his great attitude and his work ethic. Later, as a civilian physical trainer for the military in Prairie View, Texas, then at NCCU and with Olympic teams, I was able to do what Joe Walker did for me, to influence others by showing and doing. You can't just lecture; you have to teach by example. All but four of my athletes got their degrees, and those four men went into military service. It's about hard work, dedication, and education; Joe taught me the business side, what it meant to make a commitment and keep that commitment. Joe was tough, but he thought I had something special and made sure that I lived up to that potential. He opened a world to me, one that I could not have had elsewhere. He made sure that I went to the YMCA, made me understand that I had choices and freedom to make decisions, and introduced me to people who let me enjoy the finer things, like shows and the opera.

So for a boy who grew up in Harlem on the other side of 7th Avenue and 135th Street, I've been very fortunate. And I think that's why I've been so ready and willing to give whatever was needed in my community. It would be unfair to Big Momma if I hadn't listened to and accepted the leadership that I was afforded, wrong if I hadn't passed it along to my athletes. I have this theme: "Leaders succeed on the efforts of others!" So when people ask me about my coaching and my leadership, I can go down the list of individuals, athletes of mine, the All-Americans, the national champions, and the Olympians in track and field. This is a group that some people call the Walker Boys. Yes, some are Olympians: Larry Black, Edwin Moses, Abebe Bikila, Kip Keino, and Lee Calhoun. But many of these athletes have gone on to be leaders in other fields. They're businessmen, doctors, lawyers, educators.

I've been blessed to have traveled the world, to have associated with kings and presidents, to have served in positions that allowed me to cross the paths of other leaders. People know that Jesse Owens was fast, but I knew Jesse in terms of what he and his offspring have done to change the life of a community. I look with pride on my work as president of the U.S. Olympic Committee, with pride at my influence with the Knight Commission, a body dedicated to reconnecting college sports with the educational mission of American colleges and universities. I'm honored by the LeRoy Walker Human Performance Center at East Carolina University where we train elite athletes, coaches, trainers, and sports administrators from around the world.

But leadership isn't about bragging rights. What I always look for in others is what Dad Crawford and Joe Walker were looking for in me, that finished product in both athletics and education: the leader who will pass the baton, the one who will lead the next.

Ambassador Jeanette W. Hyde

Public Service

U.S. ambassador to seven countries in the Eastern Caribbean, businesswoman, private investor, and volunteer

Growing up in Hamptonville, nestled in the foothills of North Carolina, provided me with healthy and competitive opportunities that encouraged leadership—my family, my church, school, the 4-H Club, and other youth organizations that encouraged service and helping people. I have tried to keep the values I learned from my progressive-minded family and church as a part of my life, whether working in the community, in business, in politics or diplomacy. My father was in retail business, owning country stores, a farm, and a milling company. He was a great influence, very kind, generous, and always helping others.

Attending Wake Forest University taught me to embrace the world, and its motto—"Pro Humanitatae," meaning for the good of others, service to mankind—influenced me toward lifelong public service. I taught school, later became a social worker, and then a family court counselor prior to starting my own retail businesses in the early '70s. As a private investor I have participated in numerous start-up companies and helped to found two Raleigh banks, Triangle Bank and North State Bank.

The business gene goes back generations in my family, and since business is a people endeavor, I learned from growing up in a "store" atmosphere to have a positive attitude, to work hard, and to be accountable. I now know that this applies to politics, diplomacy, and life in general.

As my father was also an elected official in Yadkin County, I learned to love politics by going to meetings with him, listening to speeches, working at the polls. Although women were not as active in politics in the '50s, it became a natural for me. I was somewhat ahead of my time in that respect. I remember meeting Harry Truman in 1951 at the dedication of Wake Forest University in Winston-Salem when I was a teenager, and what an impression that made. As a freshman at Wake Forest I immediately joined a political organization, and one can guess which one it was. I took seriously the issues facing our country, perhaps more so than most young people, and I was a member of the debate team. Never having chosen to run for elected office, I have always worked to help people in whom I believed to be elected.

There have been many statesmen who have been influential leaders in my life; Governor Jim Hunt, President Bill Clinton, and Vice President Al Gore come immediately to mind. Ours is a participatory democracy and I consider it a civic responsibility to choose a political party and get actively involved. Politics has provided me an interesting and enjoyable avocation.

As an entrepreneurial businesswoman, I feel fortunate to be able to give back to the community. Believing strongly in helping young people to get an education, I have endowed scholarships at four universities, a number helping to fund studies abroad. I know from my own experience of living for two years in Greece after graduation that it is life-changing and that it enhances one's worldview.

From my years in politics, I am pleased to have friends of different political persuasions. We may not agree but we can still be friends. A fond political story concerns Senator Jesse Helms, whose assistance I needed when President Clinton appointed me to the U.S. ambassadorship to the Eastern Caribbean. Needing the Senate Foreign Relations Committee's support of my nomination, I called on the senior member of the committee, Senator Helms, and I was in great dread since I had never supported him and he certainly had no reason to support me. However, as we met and engaged in long conversation, it was as if we were two long-lost friends. He most graciously supported my nomination, for which I will always be grateful. Though very different in our politics, we connected as people and not on a partisan basis. Our close friendship that continued astonished both his friends and mine.

It was my great privilege to serve as U.S. ambassador to seven countries in the Eastern Caribbean. I worked hard to gain cooperation on behalf of U.S. interests to enter into numerous agreements and treaties that addressed drug trafficking, international crime, banking, trade issues, as well as new extradition treaties. One of the most difficult to negotiate and reach agreement on was a drug-trafficking treaty that allows our United States Coast Guard to pursue drug traffickers into territorial waters and airspace. It was important, far-reaching, and controversial—something we had needed for years. Upon final agreement with each of the seven countries, prestigious recognition and awards for successful diplomacy were presented.

It has been most rewarding to serve my country in so many ways: in business, in the helping professions, the community, in diplomacy. I believe that we can all play important leadership roles through public service that serves our nation and the American people.

Arnold Palmer

Designs for Golf's Future

President, Arnold Palmer Enterprises, world-renowned golfer, business executive, and talented golf-course designer; Associated Press Athlete of the Decade—1960–1969

My leadership philosophy has always been very basic. I give the other person the opportunity to express themselves and then listen. Then you can respond to that person in the way that you'd like to be treated. These things, perhaps you can call them leadership skills, have been very helpful to me throughout my life—whether playing golf, negotiating a business contract, or just casually meeting someone. It's important that people understand each other, that we are aware of the other person's point of view. I've found that people are generally very receptive to a friendly greeting or a knowledgeable response to the question they may have asked. You may not have the exact answer, but if you respond in a friendly and honest way people will accept that, appreciate it, and try to help you in whatever the situation might be. My father (Deacon Palmer) was the guy who taught me this, gave me the background for what I'm talking about here. He was a very tough, but generous, person and his philosophy was similar to this.

In the golf-course design business, I have to walk a fine line and sometimes have to be willing to compromise. I delegate, but I have to make the designers and architects understand what I'm trying to accomplish with the terrain. Then I give them free rein to do it their way. If they don't do it to my satisfaction or in a way that suits my philosophy, then as a leader I have to find a way to soften my criticism and not disillusion them. I want to make sure that they are able to do what I have in mind in their own creative way. If I take that creativity away from them, then I will hurt the effectiveness of the team.

As to the changes in equipment and the designing of golf courses, I will continue to be outspoken with the so-called management of golf, the USGA and the Royal and Ancient, the people who set the standards of a game that we are going to play for years and years to come. Somewhere along the way, we are going to have to stop and realize that we can't build golf courses that are 8,000 yards long just to accommodate the game's big hitters. These young people are going to continue to get stronger and, considering the modern golf ball and the modern technology in the building of golf clubs, we are going to be faced with a situation where we just won't have enough real estate to contain the game. From the design perspective, we have to stay somewhere in the range we're in now, the 7,200-yard golf course. The way to do that and contain these big hitters is to be very original in our course design. We can build longer par threes and add other features in our design that will make a 7,200-yard golf course one that remains a challenge for even the longest hitters. Build in certain little design characteristics—bunkers, traps, etc.—that will make players think twice before they pull out their three-wood and try to hit it 300 yards to get to a par five in two. Ninety percent of the people who enjoy the game on a day-to-day basis are high handicappers, players who can't hit it that far. And this technology (hot clubs and balls) is designed to make the game easier for them. I have no problem with that. But at the same time, we as leaders have to keep all this in context. As far as the golf ball is concerned, the technology that makes the ball go further isn't going to affect a twenty-handicapped player but will affect the professional who is going to hit the ball a long way. That's what we have to look at as far as this equipment technology is concerned, look at it as it relates to the professional players.

As an ambassador for golf, I have a great concern about the long-range attitude of some of the younger players in the game today. The one thing that I tried to bring into the game over the years was the prize money, the money that today has become a standard—six million dollar tournaments and millions and millions of dollars overall. At some point, we have to create an educational leadership program for professional golfers, the young people who are coming along and winning. Tom Watson once said that he played his whole life to win seventeen million dollars in prize money, over forty years of playing hard and working hard to make a living. Today, and we've seen this happen, a young player can win the Players Championship at Ponte Vedra and never be heard from again. He can get financially sound on this tour in a hurry and then go take a club job and be set for life, just by winning a big golf tournament. To put this in perspective, I've been in this game more than five decades. My official player's money—my winnings on tour—winning sixty-two tournaments is less than two million dollars. Today's players are winning that much in one week now. We have to take a look at the monetary situation and treat it gingerly because if it gets too far out of hand, then it's going to backfire and we don't want to see that happen to this great game. That leadership training for these young players may be one of the answers.

Wendell Murphy

Trusting Others

Former president and chief executive officer, Murphy Family Farms, and chairman emeritus, Murphy Family Ventures, LLC; served in North Carolina Senate

I've said this before, but I've been blessed to have lived the American dream, and it happened because of my parents. Dad was the most honest hard-working man I've ever known. He not only taught me to work but to enjoy working.

I think you'll find most leaders are hard workers, but they have to be more. They have to be consensus-builders, team-builders, and have a great deal of confidence and trust in the people who work for and with them. Like I said, my father was the hardest-working man I've ever known. But he had to do it his way, and he had to do it himself. It was another time and that was just the way he was.

Now, back in the early 1960s, Jimmy Green, who later became North Carolina's lieutenant governor, operated a tobacco marketing warehouse; in fact, he had several. Well, my daddy ended up working for him—this was when we were children—and that job that my father took with Jimmy ended up being not only the first but one of the most important leadership opportunities of my life. Our small tobacco farm was a fairly profitable enterprise, but it was a struggle to make ends meet. We had the tobacco crop and several little livestock projects. But Daddy was uneducated and didn't know how to keep records, so it was hard for him to make better business decisions, and times were tough. And Daddy didn't believe in credit. If he didn't have the money to buy us shoes, we didn't get shoes. And there were times when we didn't have a car or a truck, so we just did the farming without.

Now, I was about fourteen years old, and they offered him a job working at Jimmy Green's tobacco market. The problem was that he would have to leave home. The market was at Chadbourn, seventy miles away. They wanted him to work the night shift, flooring the tobacco, and this job offer came right at the time we were harvesting our own crop. I'll never forget this, a moment where I guess you might say I had an opportunity to finally be a leader, to call the shots without my father looking over my shoulder. We were out in the field, suckering tobacco, a horrible job, the worst job there was on that farm, and Dad was telling me that he had this offer. But he didn't know whether to take it because he wasn't sure how we'd get the rest of our crop harvested and how mother and I would possibly manage if he was gone.

I assured him right then. I said, "Daddy, this is easy, I can do it." And so he took that job and went off and worked at the market. Of course, he gave me instructions on how to do everything. But I was ready for the challenge, again the very first time I was able to lead a group of people who worked for us without Daddy second-guessing me. So I took over; I was in charge.

And I acted just like he did!

But it worked out fine. I wasn't old enough to have a driver's license so I had to depend on the hired help who could drive, and we got it done. Daddy only worked there about eight weeks but they paid him, like, two thousand dollars that first year, more later, and that was big money, very important to our family. It was really a nice thing to have that money but it was even nicer for me to be in charge of the farm and to prove that I could lead, to prove that I could do it.

Again, my father liked to do it himself and do it his way. And to be honest about it, I developed some leadership skills from observing my father and the way he worked. I said, jokingly, that I acted just like Daddy when I got the opportunity to take over while he was gone. But I would have never nor could I have ever had the success I've had if I'd been like that. My philosophy has always been to hire the best people you can hire and then to trust them to do the work. I've always tried to hire people who knew more about the business than me, to trust them and give them the opportunity to do the work.

I think leaders need to have good self-esteem, to have confidence in themselves. We all like encouragement and compliments, but timing can be very important and we have to be able to know what's right, do it, and sometimes do it without a push or pat on the back. Like I said, I know my daddy loved me, but I don't ever remember him telling me that. Neither do I ever remember him finding a lot of good in what I was doing; there was never a lot to brag about. Daddy died at the age of 70. He'd been sick for several years, and he still wanted to be in charge when he wasn't able, and we worked around that. Then on Father's Day, 1990, we were at the beach and Daddy was so weak that he could hardly get around. We'd just had a recent financial report from our business, and I took this report to him, and like I said, we'd never agreed on anything about how to run the business, and it seemed like we were always at odds. So I had this very profitable report, and as it turned out, this was just several days before he died. He looked at that financial report and said, "Well, I guess somebody's doing something right."

Colonel Curtis L. Brown, Jr., USAF (R)

Something Worth Doing Is Worth Overdoing

Former NASA astronaut, veteran of six space flights and spacecraft commander on three, logging more than 1,383 hours in space

I'm a military guy and when you're dealing with the military, the leadership is pretty structured. My philosophy in life has always been to do the right thing, and a thing that's worth doing is worth overdoing. This was taught to me by my mother and dad and has guided me through my whole career—from military pilot to being an astronaut. I've been through a number of schools that demand leadership—test pilot school, fighter weapons instructor course, and the Air Force's version of Top Gun. The idea that a thing worth doing is worth overdoing helped me graduate at the top of every class I attended in the military. When I applied to be an astronaut, they had over 5,000 applicants, and they wound up taking thirteen people. From that group, they took six pilots, and I was one of them. I had always been number one in everything I did, but there at NASA, I definitely wasn't the top dog anymore. So I really learned to listen. To survive you had to know what was important to the task. It was there that I learned that you don't lead by management, you lead by example.

On my first three missions in outer space, I was a pilot, and when you are number two in command, you sit in what we call the right seat. You really don't have a chance to lead because the commander is in charge and dictates how everything is going to run. So on those missions I decided to be the best right seater

that I could be. I did that on the first mission, followed the old "anything that's worth doing is worth overdoing," and had a very good mission, got the highest marks as a pilot. But I wasn't named commander until my fourth mission, and this was quite a blow to my ego. When I finally got that first command—this was in 1997—I got to set the rules, and as a leader working with astronauts, it's not like you have to motivate them. They're like herding kitty cats, and the toughest thing you have to do is hold them back because everybody on the crew wants to do everything. Everyone is like, "I can do it better," so that's kind of unique, and you have to be able to control the egos and the people.

As commander on that first mission, I did a really good job and so my next mission—this was 1998—was a very important one, a nine-day mission where the crew supported a variety of research payloads, including deployment of the Spartan solar-observing spacecraft, the Hubble Space Telescope Orbital Systems Test Platform, and investigations on space flight and the aging process. Well, before that flight they called me into the office and said, "You have another crew member. Senator John Glenn is going to fly with you." And for a leadership seminar, that was a laboratory. I studied and worried about how to handle that command. Here I had John Glenn on my crew, a senator, famous former astronaut, the first man to orbit the earth back in '62. He is used to leading, has this aura about him, and I'm supposed to be the commander or leader. So it was quite a leadership challenge. Now, when Senator Glenn came down to meet with me and the crew, we went through all the pleasantries and then I said, "Senator, we need to go and have a talk." And he said, "Yes, we do!" I kind of cringed when he said that because I didn't know which way the conversation was going to go. We went into another room; I closed the door and said, "Please have a seat." I remained standing, trying to take the

dominant position, then said, "We need to talk about a few things before we get into the training and the mission." And Senator Glenn said, "Wait a minute. Can I go first?" And he said, "My name is John Glenn, and I'm payload specialist number II [and that means the lowest-ranking person on the flight]. My job on this flight is to do some medical research, and you're the boss. If I'm not doing a good job or studying hard enough or carrying my weight on this crew, your job is to kick me in the butt until I get all my work done. I expect you to do that. Feel free to push me as hard as you can. I'm proud to be a member of your crew." And I said, "Well, I really can't think of anything to add to that. I just wanted to make sure that you understood that I was the commander and that you are the payload specialist because we have all these roles to carry out."

We had a very good mission; he did a great job, we got home safely, and today, I laugh about that and say that I'm so glad that Curt Brown's name isn't a part of a TV *Jeopardy* answer under the category of LEADERSHIP: "The NASA commander responsible for the death of John Glenn."

Later, in John Glenn's book, he wrote about this mission and called my leadership style "Laid-back, but very much in control." That was quite a compliment because I don't like to micromanage. I expect people to be professional and take care of their responsibilities. But as a leader, I would always make changes when necessary. In a spacecraft, everything has to be done right. It can't be second-rate, and a thing worth doing is worth overdoing.

Mary Duke Biddle Trent Semans

Appreciating the Arts

Leading North Carolina philanthropist, supporting education and arts programs across the state; continued the Duke University founding family's legacy of philanthropic contributions to the community

I wonder how many people know who the late Robert Lee Humber was? Robert Humber was the absolute key to the establishment of the new North Carolina Museum of Art. He was an attorney from Greenville who had a big oil container business in France at the end of World War II. He later served as a state legislator, was passionate about paintings and art, and determined that he was going to take the money he made abroad and establish a museum. In 1924, the N.C. Art Society was formed to promote a state art museum in Raleigh. Robert Phifer of New York, originally from North Carolina, left his fine painting collection and funds toward a gallery. Gradually, the state took on more and more responsibility, and when Senator Humber was successful in approaching Samuel Kress about funds and donating part of his collection to the public institution, the museum was well on its way. Mr. Humber came to talk to many of us about this idea, and one could just tell that the man was a leader who would do anything to get this museum of art off the ground. The rest is history. The museum in the old Highway Building in Raleigh was opened. Then, they were able to bring in the prestigious Wilhelm Reinhold Valentiner, known as William in the States, as the first director. Valentiner was a key player in what has now grown into that wonderful Museum of Art in Raleigh on Blue Ridge Road. But the fact is this: the vision and leadership of Robert Humber made us focus on the arts.

Now, the story of the North Carolina School of the Arts begins with Terry Sanford, a great leader and a creative man. Terry, who was the governor at the time, brought a brilliant writer, John Ehle, to his staff. John was a novelist at the University of North Carolina in Chapel Hill. Terry called on him and asked, "I understand that you are a very imaginative person. What aren't we doing for the people in this state?" One of his responses was, "We don't have any professional training for professional artists. There may be truck drivers out there who could have been oboists but never had a chance to play. Let me take you to Vittorio Giannini; he has some incredible ideas along these lines." So off they went to visit Giannini, who had taught at Juilliard and Curtis and was, at the time, at the Brevard Music Camp. When they arrived, they learned that Vittorio was in the hospital having just suffered a heart attack. When Dr. Giannini learned who his guests were and that they wanted to talk about his idea for a state school for the arts, well, Giannini sat up in bed, and he talked all day. Today, a lot of people still refer to the school as Giannini's Dream . . . a dream that would become a training ground for students from middle school through graduate school for professional careers now in music, dance, drama, design and production, and film. Terry Sanford bought Giannini's vision completely, appointed a board, and called my Jim, Dr. James Semans (a world-renowned urologist and Duke University professor). Then later, Jim was asked to accept the chairmanship. Well, this was a big decision, and Jim and I met with John Ehle at a restaurant called the Ranch House in Chapel Hill. There was conversation. I thought it was perfect for him and encouraged him. Jim wasn't just a great leader and great doctor, he had a tremendous passion for the arts, and I promised to assist him in any way I could. He remained in that position as chairman of the board for some fifteen years. We had a great time doing this together. It was just one of those very fortuitous things. He wanted to know the students and faculty and was very much involved in making another one of Giannini's ideas a reality, an idea for an international program. Over the past thirty years, that program has taken student orchestras from the school to Europe to train and perform. Governor Dan Moore and his wife, Jeanelle, who became one of my best friends, kicked it off with a grand celebration at the Governor's Mansion. We contributed to it, as did the Kenans and others. Yes, the money was important, but there was a lot more to all of this for us than the funding. We had always had a tremendous passion for the arts. And the night we sat at that Ranch House in Chapel Hill and talked to John Ehle about this school and the role that Jim and I might play, well, we could never have imagined what all this would become. But the success is clearly a story of leadership, with many people making significant contributions to the creation of just what North Carolina needed, a real conservatory for the arts for professionally destined students.

David H. Murdock

To Do the Impossible You Must See the Invisible

Chairman and owner of numerous privately held companies including Castle & Cooke, Inc., and Dole Food Company, Inc., a Fortune 500 company which is the world's largest producer and marketer of high-quality fresh fruit, fresh vegetables, and fresh-cut flowers; constructed the North Carolina Research Campus, a high-tech life science research center dedicated to the betterment of the world's health and nutrition, a more than one billion dollar investment

When asked about the leadership that led to the creation of the North Carolina Research Campus here in Kannapolis, I often refer to a belief of mine—to do the impossible you must see the invisible. I love creativity; the mundane, even if it's nice, doesn't really interest me. Most things that I want to do are impossible or would seem to be. So I'm always busy looking for the invisibility—what might be, what can be, and then putting it all together. My definition of leadership, and this applies to the creation of the Research Campus, is that to lead you must be in front. You can't be a leader if you're walking behind other people. I always say, "I'm number one." And I don't mean that in an egotistical way, although some would think that it sounds that way. But if you are going to do something important and you're going to do something important and you're following, that's all you're doing, following

someone who did something of value. I'd been blessed with success and wanted to invest in a continuing thing rather than giving money out hither and yon. So this research campus was the answer. The opportunity was here in Kannapolis, North Carolina, when Cannon (textiles) went up for sale. I made a bid and bought the property. I decided that I would build a research campus, one that would focus on important health-oriented research. Leaders have the ability to make strong decisions. I was spending my own money so I wanted everything to be perfect. I thought that if it's worth doing, do it perfectly. My formula for success here and in other endeavors is very simple: I see an opportunity, come up with the solution, and then do it. Perhaps that might be called leadership. Most people can see opportunity but very few can come up with the solution. An even smaller number can execute it. This scientific community is a good example. It will be a place where the best minds will shape the way we understand nutrition and its relationship to disease.

Sixty percent of the people in this country are overweight, 40 percent are obese. I've been a fish vegetarian for many years so I wanted to create a place that would solve people's health problems—from state-of-the-art laboratories to medical facilities that will treat patients. There will be a rehabilitation and exercise component and a major health center that teaches good eating habits. Again, I enjoy the creativity. As a developer, I've built shopping centers and thousands of homes, so I've been involved in the entire project here, from the Regency architecture, which is a favorite of mine, to the furnishings. All of this is very important to the creation of this campus.

As to the leadership? Well, unless you know how to make things happen you can't lead. So I brought in the leadership of North Carolina, a state, by the way, that I have a special place

for in my heart. Senator Marc Basnight carried the torch for this project and Senator Fletcher Hartsell was also very helpful. Molly Broad, who was then the president of the university system, and Erskine Bowles, who followed her in that position, were both extremely encouraging. While visiting the different universities, I met with scientists from a great variety of disciplines and interests. Pretty soon we were putting something together that would work for everyone. As the campus became more of a reality, we gained more support. The core lab is the heart of the campus, and we needed a great core lab to attract other companies here. My company, Dole Foods, will have a building; Pepsi Cola and many other well-known companies are coming in. All the state universities are involved, with NC State, the University of North Carolina–Chapel Hill, and Duke University playing major roles.

It was my desire to build a scientific center second to none. I think we have done that with our core lab. The core lab will house some of the greatest scientists in the world, functioning with the greatest scientific equipment. We have a multi-million dollar 950 megahertz nuclear magnetic resonance (NMR) machine. It's one of a kind, the largest in existence, with the capability to study things that no one has ever been able to study, go further and in greater depth. These studies will impact a great number of areas of medicine.

When I'm asked where this idea for the research campus came from I say, "Well, I daydreamed this up." That's the way I function, and this daydreaming is one of the best abilities that I have as a leader. To do the impossible you must see the invisible, be a daydreamer. What I see here is the invisible—a day when breakthroughs in science on this campus will impact the well-being of so many people through science, research that will help us better understand nutrition and its relationship to disease.

Congressman Bob Etheridge

Working Harder to Accomplish a Common Goal

Serves on the U.S. House Agriculture, Budget, and Homeland Security Committees; chairman of the Subcommittee on General Farm Commodities and Risk Management of the House Agriculture Committee; served eight years as North Carolina's elected superintendent of public instruction

Some people say leaders are born. I'm not sure that's totally true. Sometimes leadership is acquired through relationships and sometimes through circumstances, from the environment you may find yourself in at any given moment. You will see people who go through a career, and then there it is, one certain moment comes and leadership surfaces.

For me, I had an opportunity to play basketball at Campbell University as a walk-on. They didn't come looking for me. I came looking for them because I enjoyed the game and really needed money to get through college. So I literally earned a scholarship, and then wound up as co-captain of the team, which was a leadership position. It wasn't easy, a lot of hard work, and hard work is a key ingredient to leadership. There's a commonality to leaders, a willingness to work harder to hone a skill or to accomplish a common goal. That was so in my case. I didn't have the most talent, but I wasn't going to be outworked by anyone, and that's been true in whatever I've attempted to do. When I was a county commissioner in Harnett County, we worked extremely hard and accomplished a lot of things—built the first new schools in fifty years, put in water

systems, built an airport—and that was all in four years of service.

Leaders don't accomplish all that on their own. We have to convince a lot of people to join us and, more often than not, we have to get those people out of their comfort zones. That's the toughest part, enabling others to lead. You must sell them on your vision. Once they buy in, they have ownership. When they have ownership, you can step back. That was the case in Harnett County, and today it has those schools, the airport, and more miles of water line than probably any county in the state.

Leadership isn't necessarily what you do as an individual, it's what you set in motion that will continue after you've moved on. So my view is clearly that leadership is about empowering people. That's what I've tried to do throughout my career—whether it was when I was chairman of the Appropriations Committee in the North Carolina General Assembly or representing the state in Congress in Washington. When I served as superintendent of schools in North Carolina, we made major changes, and the key word here is "we." We developed a whole new assessment of secondary education for the state, revamped the curriculum. We developed and implemented one of the first measurement instruments in the country, giving North Carolina the ability to measure what was being taught as it applied to learning. None of that was done alone. You can't touch everything yourself. There are a limited amount of things that any leader can do. Leaders enable, get the ball rolling, then step back and let other capable people push that ball forward.

Now, if you're talking about leadership in Congress, then the one thing that you learn in a hurry is that you're dealing with a lot of people who have pretty big egos. They wouldn't be there otherwise. Many are committee chairmen and have their own ideas about things. So one of the keys to leadership there is the un-

derstanding that other people have things that they just absolutely are going to have to have. You're not just dealing with the whole country. There are many regional issues. So you have to find out where everyone really needs to be, and then it becomes a matter of compromise, figuring out how to make things work. But in the end, it has to be fair to all parties and fair to the country and the taxpayers. Now, that's the way we were able to get the farm bill passed this time—leadership. And it wasn't easy, not easy at all.

People expect their leaders to work hard. For some, this comes easier than others. I grew up on a tobacco farm in Johnston County, and so I've always known that work was a key ingredient to leadership and a key to success. Whether playing a sport, public service, or business, nobody was going to outwork me. If you grow up on a farm as I did, you get to do a lot of things, from milking a cow to feeding hogs, priming tobacco, picking corn. And you learn to work. Today farms are specialized, but back then we learned a lot of skills. I used to tell folks when I went to school that I had a lot of experience but not as much learning as I needed. So leaders have to be open to learning, willing to get their hands dirty, and then, ultimately, do the right thing. If you take shortcuts, it will catch up with you. Someone once said to me, "Well, you've had a lot of opportunities and been somewhat successful—county commissioner, state legislator, state superintendent of schools, a U.S. congressman, nineteen years in business, a family that's doing well." Here's what I said: "Listen, I'm blessed. But I've never believed I had a position. I've always had a job." People who have jobs work, and if you'll work at whatever you do, be inclusive, try to do the right thing, and don't worry about who gets all the credit, you'll feel good at the end of the day. And to a great extent, that's what leadership is all about.

Donna Chavis

Doing Good with What You Have

Executive director, NCGives; served as chief operating officer, Center for Community Action, and as executive director, Native Americans in Philanthropy; founding board member of the Changemakers Fund, serving as co-chair for two years

I grew up in Pembroke, North Carolina, in a Native American family in my old family home. My father was ill when I was young, and my momma cleared the stumps off the land to help build that house.

There were two kinds of Indians in Pembroke—brick-house Indians and outhouse Indians. We were outhouse Indians because we didn't have indoor plumbing. When I was a child, my father was a small-appliance repairman—radios, stoves, refrigerators, and TVs—and at a very young age he became sick with a terminal illness. He had a heart condition and cancer. He couldn't work in a public way but he did work for the community, and we didn't have much of a financial base. But he taught me a lesson in leadership that has stuck with me to this day, really led me to the career path in grassroots philanthropy for underrepresented communities. He always made himself available to the community, especially the senior citizens. He trained Momma, and between the two of them, they could fix just about anything.

Now, when I was a little girl, it seemed like he was gone every Christmas. As a child you buy into all the traditions about families, and sometimes the week before Christmas, Daddy would be gone until past midnight. I was the one that it really upset because we were so close.

He would take the children with him as much as he could because he wanted us to experience what he did for the community—there were seven girls and one boy who survived out of the fourteen children that Momma had. So this one Christmas, he took me with him and we were going down the road to an elder's home. He was going to fix her oven and he said, "You know I just can't let these little ladies be without their cakes on Christmas; they have to have their ovens to bake."

And it was then that I knew that he was teaching me that I shouldn't be so upset about him being gone because this was his way of giving. Then he said it, the line that has stuck with me about leadership my whole life. He said, "You know, girl, it's not what you have that counts. It's what you do with what you have." He told me that we didn't have much, but what we had, we could share. I was around the third or fourth grade and that marked my life.

It was funny, but when Daddy passed away we found an old ledger book of his, and he'd written down everything he'd ever repaired. We laughed and said, "You know if he'd gotten paid for all this, we wouldn't have been poor."

But we weren't poor. We'd learned that giving is more important, and I think it shaped all of our lives. He had the great gift of leadership, not just the talent to fix things but to do it for the community. That's the major message that I received about leadership, and I've been able to connect it to my life along the way, working as a grassroots leader with underrepresented communities.

Fortunately, Daddy was still alive when this happened. And he got quite a kick out of this. We took our lunches to school because we couldn't afford cafeteria lunches. This was before the free-lunch program. So all we could afford were the sandwich spreads—mayonnaise, relish—and that's what we had for lunch every day. A piece of bread with mayonnaise or relish spread. The students who went to the cafeteria and had lunch were always coming back and complaining that the food was bad. They were going on and on. I started to feel sorry for these students, so I organized all of us who brought our lunches to share. So one day when they came back from the lunch room they had our little sandwiches on their desks, which we thought were really good.

Not a big hit. Of course later, I realized that they were just spoiled rotten. And then in a few years when we all had a lunch program, and we got the school lunches, I was just thrilled. I thought, "What in the world is wrong with this food?"

I've thought of this many times since—that was one of the first times that I remembered what my daddy had said: "It's not what you have, it's what you do with what you have!" And you know, sharing our lunches with the kids who were complaining about the hot meals in our school may have been the first thing that I ever organized. The thing is that in leadership so often these deficit communities get so caught up in the need that it becomes apparent that they just don't have the time to do all they need to do. But what I say about foundation work—philanthropy—is if you think of time, talent, and treasure, there will always be enough time and talent but as to money, well, there will never be enough of that to solve all our problems. But we should always have enough time to use our talent. And so I guess that I'd be very flattered to hear anyone say that I grew up to be a lot like my daddy—someone who had enough time for others. I've tried to be his kind of leader in these underrepresented communities, in a sense—out there helping them fix their small appliances.

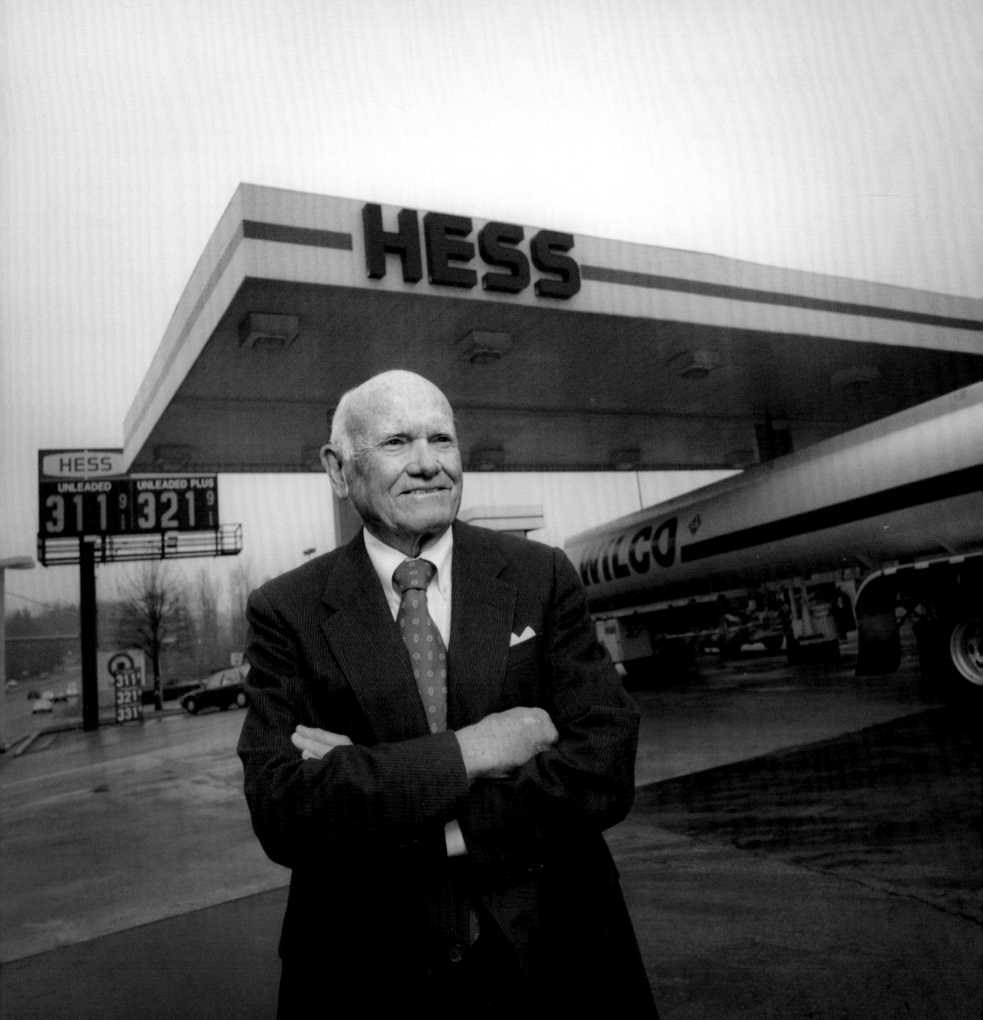

Tab Williams

A Lasting Work Ethic

Created A.T. Williams Oil Company, which became Wilco Travel and Fuel Plazas, the largest independent gasoline retailer in North Carolina

I wouldn't be where I am today if it weren't for my father's farm in Pitt County, where I learned to work. Then NC State gave me an education that afforded me some real choices and career opportunities.

I was the oldest of four children, born in '27, and my dad was a tenant farmer. We didn't have inside plumbing, and we had to furnish most of the food we ate. But it was there on that farm that I learned to work and to enjoy the work. Tobacco was king bee back then. If you didn't have a good crop, you suffered. One of the valuable lessons that I learned from my father, something that served me well later in the oil business, was to diversify. Those who depended solely on tobacco could be ruined by hail or drought. But my father diversified, he grew cucumbers and potatoes. We raised chickens and sold them and sold the eggs as well.

The best way to explain how much I treasure the experience of working on that farm is to say that, all things being equal, if two people applied for a job with my company today, and one had a farming background and one didn't, I would choose the farmer because the person who lives on a farm has to know how to solve problems, has to work, and develop a vision for how to make things work.

When I went to NC State, I decided to major in agriculture because that's all I knew. I remembered the extension service; Roy Bennett, our extension agent, was quite an influence on me, a real leader in our lives. This was during a time when so many different diseases were killing tobacco crops—black shank, Granville wilt, blue mold—and the College of Agriculture and Life Sciences at NC State was doing a lot of important research, and Roy brought us the results. I remember the first time we tried the resistant plants. Our crop grew while our neighbors' failed. That was a big impression on me about NC State, how they were leaders in research and how that research helped us save our tobacco crop.

I convinced my father that I should go to NC State and told him that I thought I could get by—books, tuition, food—on a thousand dollars, and coming from where I came from, well, I knew how to make it work. Now, when I went to NC State I wasn't prepared to be there, to compete with the kids who had gone to the larger high schools in the state. But I didn't begrudge the hard work and graduated. Today the A.T. Williams Oil Company, which is the parent company of Wilco Convenience Stores, operates more than three hundred gas stations and stores. We have a great number of employees, and that's the message that I give to them, that if you have a passion for your work and you like something, give it 100 percent, and use good judgment—chances are, it's going to work.

When I left NC State, there was a job waiting for me. I had majored in agronomy, and I worked as an extension agent in Forsyth County. I was drafted several months later—this was during the Korean War—and when I returned my job was waiting for me. I enjoyed the extension service but later took a position managing the tobacco market in Winston-Salem. This was a great experience because I learned sales, how to work with the local chambers of commerce, how to motivate people. Then my father-in-law, Roby Taylor, asked me if I'd like to join him and his two sons in the oil business. I loved it, managed about six stores for several years, but realized that it would be best for me and my late wife, Lib, to branch out on our own. She had some stock in the company and owned three stations herself, so we started the Wilco Oil business—three stores, and, now, my son Steve is running the company and we have more than three hundred.

In those early years, I just had a secretary and a delivery truck driver; the phone was connected at the house so that if no one answered it would be picked up there, so it was very much a hard-working family partnership. My first wife, Lib, passed away a number of years ago but it's the same today with my new wife, Linda, a family partnership. We've now merged a joint venture with Amerada Hess, another oil company with a substantial East Coast presence. Hess had been our supplier from almost the beginning, and my son Steve guided this transaction. I never thought much about how big the company might get, but never forgot that lesson that I learned from my father—sometimes you have to diversify. In business if you don't grow, you risk sliding backwards. We realized that we couldn't sit still as more and more of the big-box retailers threatened to get into the gasoline business just as a loss leader. So we've had to get with the trends, meet the needs of our customers by making a number of our stores convenience stores—one-stop shopping. The latest trend is the partnership between our stores and fast food restaurants: Wendy's, Subway, Taco Bell, and Krispy Kreme.

So it worked. And I guess that's been the key, that word "work." I always liked challenges, and from that time when I worked on the farm, my daddy always gave us goals, and if we reached our goals then we got rewarded. I follow that same principle today with this company. I guess if there's any secret to success it's simply this: you have to like what you do and if you do there's no work to it.

Edward M. Gore, Sr.

Developing a Dream

Real-estate entrepreneur; co-founded

Sunset Beach with his father, Mannon

C. Gore, and developed award-winning

Sunset Beach golf communities, Sea Trail

and Ocean Ridge Plantations

On my first day of school, our teacher had placed little twelve-inch rulers on those old wooden desks of ours. Written on those gifts was the golden rule, "Do unto others as you would have them do unto you." Well, this wasn't the first time I heard that rule because my father, Mannon Gore, had instilled that in all of us kids.

That was the way he lived and the way he did business. He farmed just about ten miles from what is now Sunset Beach, the town that he would develop and take the leadership role in creating. This was back in the early 1950s. He'd reached a plateau in farming. It was no longer a challenge, and he was making a good living, and it was at that point that he said he could just feel it in his bones. The time was right to diversify. He started out with a partner, Odell Williamson, and they bought the six miles of land that's now Ocean Isle. Having been in the Coast Guard, Dad had the wherewithal in his life experiences, working with dredges on the Ohio River, to know how to do things. He wasn't educated as an engineer, but he'd learned through observation.

They got the access to the island and built a sand-clay base and sold numerous lots. Dad and Odell were both strong-willed men and, one day, Dad just decided that the partnership wasn't going to work, so he made an offer to buy or sell. Odell decided to buy, and so Dad turned his eyes toward Sunset Beach.

He was early into the development when I came home from the service in 1958 and joined him in the business. My wife, Dinah, and I married in '59. I'd gone to Campbell, then to East Carolina. I took over the construction aspect, and having been a business major, I took his general journal and made a separate set of books so he and my sister Barbara could use these books and post contracts, which were numerous.

When I look at Sunset Beach today, it's hard not to remember those early years—the risks he took to buy additional land that was necessary, the dredging, the surveying, the challenge of the financing. There was only one bank during those early years and a lot of politics in that bank, so it took some real leadership skills, using option sales as safety nets. He had to find outside lending sources to make this dream of his happen.

My father had so many of the skills that make an excellent leader. He was congenial, liked by people, but what I saw and carried over into my career was his work ethic and the willingness to seize the moment. As a father and partner, he talked to me about sad family legacies and how there were so many of these wealthy upper-class people who had opportunities but never built on their parents' and grandparents' dreams.

That became a goal for me, to fulfill the dream he had for Brunswick County and Sunset Beach, and in doing so, being a good environmental caretaker. I guess it was ingrained in me because when my dad retired, Dinah and I bought the company. In 1976, I was able to acquire more land from the International Paper Company. I'd borrowed my limit and had to bring in partners. I chose men that I knew to help me get others, and this partnership led to the development of Sea Trail Plantation. Later, we did the same thing at Ocean Ridge Plantation.

Dad set the example of taking the risk, which was not always easy. And Dinah and I had some tough decisions to make. She was a great partner, one who would always voice her opinion but never say no. My father had never finished high school; he went to work on the farm. But when it came to my going to college, there was never a question. He encouraged me to go, and it is through his leadership and our good fortune that Dinah and I have been able to support initiatives at NC State University and Campbell University—scholarships and endowments that will help develop the skills that the Shelton Leadership Center promotes.

If my father were here today, I know he'd be proud of Sunset Beach, his legacy, and all that we'll attempt to do here in the future. But he'd look at it all in the light of the values-based leadership rules that he lived by and that I've tried to live by, which is exemplified by the Four-Way Test of the Rotary:

- Is it the truth?
- Is it fair to all concerned?
- Will it build good will and better friendships?
- Will it be beneficial to all concerned?

Richard Petty

A Victory Junction

Won a record 200 NASCAR races and NASCAR Championship seven times; a "founding father" of Victory Junction Gang Camp for children with chronic medical conditions and serious illnesses

The Victory Junction Gang Camp is a year-round camp that serves kids, ages seven to fifteen, with a variety of health issues. These are kids who wouldn't be able to attend a camp because of their medical needs. During the summer, we offer week-long, disease-specific sessions with up to 125 kids per session. During the fall, winter, and spring, there are family weekends.

Here's the deal. It's taken a lot of leadership to make this a reality. But if you go back, it really all started with my grandson, Adam, who died tragically in a race accident in New Hampshire.

When Adam started driving he was always visiting hospitals, talking to kids his age or younger. Here was this nineteen-year-old who was interested in other kids. One summer, he and his mom and dad—Kyle and Pattie—drove from Daytona over to Boggy Creek, Florida, where Paul Newman had one of his Hole in the Wall Gang camps for kids. Adam said, "You know, it would be neat if we could do something like this in our part of the country." When they came back to North Carolina we talked about this, this was right before Adam was killed. There was some land for sale up beside his father's property in Trinity, North Carolina. And so here's this teenager who has nothing except a future as a driver and the money that he might earn going to banks and offering to sign over all of his future winnings to pay for the land that would be this camp for kids. Then there was the tragedy, his death. Of course, we were all just stunned, devastated. So we put that whole idea on hold. Then, maybe three or four months later, Kyle and Pattie came to me and said, "Look, we'd like to get something started on that camp. It was one of Adam's dreams and we'll do it in his memory."

So Adam was the visionary. His mom and dad took the lead, and pretty soon, we were going to a lot of big hospitals, asking questions, learning that there were like 250,000 children in our general area who could use a camp like this—kids with every affliction from arthritis, asthma, and cancer to burns, cystic fibrosis, diabetes, and autism. The original plan was to offer the camp to people from Richmond, Virginia, to South Carolina, to cover this section of the country, take care of these kids who couldn't go to a regular camp. Kyle had raced with Paul Newman, and so he knew him and he knew of us. And once Paul got wind of our interests, he called the people at his Hole in the Wall Gang camps and said, "Help them." We learned a lot from them, what to do and what not to do.

So many people have been involved in what we have here today, so many leaders. I said, "Well, we'll give you some land." This was on the backside of our property here in Randolph County, about sixty-five acres. I think we bought an additional ten acres. Then, we just took this idea for the camp to the leadership of the racing community, to our sponsors, to our fans. NASCAR got behind it, and of course, the drivers joined in. And today, you can see the dozens of bright-colored buildings with the drivers' and race teams' names on them—the Goody's Body Shop Medical Center, the Hendrick Motorsports Fuel Stop, the Michael Waltrip Operation Marathon Sports Center.

All we had was an idea. What made this work was that so many people—the counselors, the hundreds of volunteers, the contributors—gravitated to the camp because of one thing: it's about helping kids. Kyle and Pattie just jumped in and took Adam's dream and made it become a reality. I wander around on the outside and try to keep them all together, do whatever I can to keep it going. We try to keep this low-key for the kids, but this is really a hospital with camping functions surrounding it. Goody's Headache Powder, who we've been working with for years, gave us the first million dollars to start the hospital. That was one of the first things we built. And when the kids come, we don't tell them it's a hospital, they've had enough of that. We call it the Body Shop. So when they get here, they can enjoy a new sense of life for the first time. So many of them have been excluded from the real world. All they've heard is, "You can't do this and you can't do that, can't fish, can't swim, can't ride a horse, can't rope climb." They come here, and they do all of those things and more. The experience can be the biggest week of their life. What this place really does is this: it opens the rest of the world to them. When they go back home and someone says, "You can't do this and can't do that," they can say, "Well, I did that at the Victory Junction Gang Camp, and I can do it again."

I could never have imagined seeing what we have here today, this little Disneyland for these very special kids. Now, there are people in Kansas who want us to do the same thing, create another camp for kids out there. When I look at this land that I played on as a healthy kid and see these kids who aren't healthy playing on it today, well, it's very special. The good Lord blessed us with four healthy children and twelve healthy grandchildren. I just think of the Victory Junction Gang Camp as payback time.

Julius L. Chambers

Justice for All

Opened first integrated law practice in North Carolina, which influenced evolving federal civil-rights law more than any other practice in the United States; former director counsel of the NAACP Legal Defense and Education Fund; former chancellor of North Carolina Central University

I've seen a number of people exercise great leadership over the years. I remember leaving North Carolina and going to New York to work with the NAACP Legal Defense Fund. I was interested in making a good first impression on Jack Greenberg, who was the director counsel. I wanted to let Jack and his associate director, Connie Motley, know what I could do. I worked all night on a petition for certiorari search that would be presented to the Supreme Court for review. The case was from Atlanta, Georgia, and had to do with the desegregation of schools. This would have been in the early 1960s, and I was confident that I'd pulled together a number of cases that would make good arguments and move the Court to agree to review our petition. Now, Connie had been handling the case and, well, she and Jack looked at this initial certiorari search petition of mine that I was so proud of and just ripped it apart. Now, what I learned about leadership was this: it's about people committed to a cause and those providing leadership better be prepared to do what they need to do, to do the right thing, do it right. They had the leadership skills to make their criticisms constructive and make the experience a good one.

There was another experience involving Vernon Jordan, one where I saw values-based leadership in action. Vernon was the president of the National Urban League; this was during Jimmy Carter's presidency. Vernon had gone to Washington for this national meeting and had made some comments that had gotten him into some hot water. He'd been very critical of President Carter because he didn't think the president had taken a forceful enough stand in a racial matter, one that dealt with schools. The president expressed his displeasure. So Vernon needed to bring some people together in a hurry to support his comments. He sent out emergency telegrams to a number of black leaders and civil-rights organizations, asking us to come together to support him on this issue. I was director counsel of the NAACP Defense Fund, so we—black leaders with some very diverse opinions and not a very unified group—came together to meet with Vernon on the issue. A number of opinions were expressed; the conversations became quite heated. But I watched Vernon work with the heads of these organizations, and what he did was talk to us about the more pervasive problem that minorities across the country were facing. And by taking that tack, he was able to unify this group in a way that was quite impressive.

Another instance of leadership was in the early '70s when I was litigating the Charlotte-Mecklenburg Schools case, a case that was aimed at moving the Supreme Court to uphold busing to achieve desegregation in the Charlotte area. We had a community in an uproar, blacks were in an uproar, concerned about the whites in regard to the integration of the schools; whites were concerned about the advocacy of blacks on this very volatile issue. C. D. Spangler, who was the vice-chairman of the school board here at that time, stepped forward and brought the warring factions together to talk. This was very positive and a major step. Others that showed incredible leadership were Maggie Ray and Sarah Stevenson. Sarah was black and worked with a pretty active black group. Maggie was white and worked with a citizens' advisory group, young white people. The two of them agreed to a common goal, to help the school system come up with a plan that would help solve the issues of cross-town busing, which was key to this case. The result was an agreement that made a major impact on accomplishing the goal of desegregation as it applied to the busing issues.

If there's an issue today that's still very much in need of leadership it's that decision to promote integration of the schools, gaining a better understanding of the real value of diversity. The challenge that's still very much here: we make progress one year and retreat the next. Quite honestly, what's most frightening about all of this is that we are at the point now where we could be losing ground, at a place where all that we've accomplished in integration might be going backward. This issue needs leadership, someone to step in to talk across communities, to talk about the value of diversity, the value of bringing all people—people with diverse ethnicity—together. I hope we have that leader now, one who will promote a better understanding of the real value of diversity.

William Harrison

Reality-Based Leadership

Former chairman and chief executive officer, JPMorgan Chase & Co.; spent entire career with JPMorgan Chase and the lead architect of one of the largest global banks in the business

I'm just a great believer in leadership, and what I've said to our hundred thousand employees here at JPMorgan Chase is that everybody can be a leader.

I define leadership as having a view, a willingness to express that view or vision, and then the ability to influence people to make the changes that will make the company better. Leaders have different qualities and different experiences. But here are some core qualities of leadership that I think are important: along with the vision, leaders must be authentic, know who they are. If they try to be something that they're not, they will probably fail. They have to be secure, comfortable in their own skins, and they need to be able to confront reality. Leaders face things every day that they might want to put off. But confronting the reality of a situation is absolutely critical. If you are the CEO of a bank, and there's a major consolidation trend in the industry that's been going on for some time, that's the reality. You can't sit back. You've got to confront that reality, perhaps get out and acquire or merge with another bank. You have to do whatever it takes to make your company successful. Great leaders have excellent interpersonal skills; they relate well to people. If they want to make something happen, they've got to be able to get their people behind them, because change

or progress is not a unilateral action. Attitude is paramount. You can't look at things in a Pollyannaish way, but people want to be around leaders who are positive. If you have a team, then you don't want people with bad attitudes on that team. It brings the company down.

Good leaders are open, honest, direct, and lastly, leaders have to deliver. I've been involved in a number of mergers and buyouts, and these transactions are never easy. I think mergers are the ultimate challenge of leadership. When you put two companies together, on day one it is chaos. The board of directors can't command everyone to respect the new leadership, and things are moving so fast and are so challenging and uncomfortable that bringing everyone together falls in the lap of the leader. If that person isn't showing the right leadership skills on day one, they will quickly get rejected, and the result will be failure.

I was personally in the middle of a number of these mergers. Starting in 1992, we put four of the top five New York banks together. These mergers went fairly well, and I thought, this has been great. I'd learned a lot, developed as a leader, and frankly, didn't see a whole lot of challenges ahead. Then the perfect economic storm hit, the bursting of the Internet bubble. This led to chaos in the marketplace, which affected private equity business and the telecom business in a big way. Suddenly, JPMorgan Chase was being sued by all the plaintiff lawyers with Enron and WorldCom. The whole situation became very difficult, very unattractive from a reputational perspective and a financial perspective. This was the biggest challenge that I'd ever had to deal with as a CEO. Younger people would come into my office and say, "Bill, we're so sorry. This must be very difficult. How are you doing? How is the firm doing? Do we have job security?!" And I'd say,

"When I get into a really tough situation like this, I mentally fast-forward the tape, asking myself what the worst-case scenario is and can I manage it?" I've always been able to find a scenario where I could say, "Yes, I can manage this." That doesn't mean that it's a great outcome, but I can live with it and I can manage it. Then I ask myself a personal question, "What's the worst thing that could happen to me?" If I get fired, I will be sad because I won't be here to make this great company better. But I will still have had a great career, have my health, and a great family at home. So I'm fine. And then I'd tell them, "JPMorgan Chase in our worst year is going to make three billion dollars. We have an AA rating. So we're going to be fine." As a leader, you have to be able to understand that, step back and pass that message along to those who work for and with you. You have to believe in the vision, believe in the people, and just get out there and continue to work hard to make that vision happen.

Today, I feel very good about what I've been able to leave behind at JPMorgan Chase. The company is on very solid ground. Jamie Damon, my successor and the new CEO, is the right guy to take this company to the next level. So I'm very comfortable and satisfied with where the company is today and have no doubts about its future. This is very important for a leader. We can do good things while we're in office, but we're always going to feel even better if we can leave knowing that what we've helped put together there is in the best of hands and headed in the right direction.

Ann Goodnight

An Eye on Education

Leader in the establishment of Cary Academy; director of community relations at SAS Institute, world's largest privately held software company with 10,000 employees

My husband, Jim [Goodnight], and I used to sit in the evenings and talk; this was in the mid-nineties, and almost always the conversation would come to education—the challenges, and what was necessary to prepare students to compete in this incredibly competitive job market. We talked about how these students could help put North Carolina and this country in a position to compete in the world economy. We were frustrated by the way we saw public schools going, about what needed to be fixed. Then Jim said, "Heck, let's just build a school." In just two years from the development of that concept, that idea, we were opening the doors of Cary Academy. It was the creating and building of this school that made us even more aware of the need for leadership in this area—education—an emphasis on the teaching of technology, one-to-one teacher-to-student ratios, computer literacy, the mastering of relevant language skills. We also became aware of just how passionate we both were about education. Although Cary Academy was our early interest and has served as an excellent model for this kind of relevant education, over the past ten years our focus has now changed to the public schools of North Carolina. But,

again, it was the Academy and that experience that brought us to addressing education across the board in North Carolina, how critical it is for the quality of life that we want for all the children of the state. The Academy's mission is to provide an excellent college preparatory education for students. We went into this committed to maintaining a student body that reflects the diverse culture and socioeconomic backgrounds within our community. So that was the mission, but the real nut of it for me was to have a school that offered a better student-teacher relationship, with a focus on the nurturing of children. I felt like the middle schools were getting so large—fifteen hundred to two thousand students—and sensed that relationships between the student and teacher had become diluted. These middle school years are when you really have an opportunity to work with these kids; it's a very strategic point in their lives. That, along with more exposure to the arts, athletics, and academics, would be of paramount importance.

Jim, on the other hand, said, "We need to put the tools of the business world in place, teach them the technology." So he saw this as a great leadership opportunity, one that would help prepare students for jobs to compete in the real world economy.

The faculty is excellent, and because technology changes, the professional development is ongoing. There's a big emphasis on language proficiency. We decided to emphasize Chinese, French, German, and Spanish, and use native-born language teachers who speak the language in the classrooms. Our students spend two to three weeks immersed in their chosen language and in the junior year the whole class, be it Chinese or French, goes to

the countries speaking that language. We have a 100 percent graduation rate; these kids are so prepared and they just sail out of here. When they get into colleges and universities, they are often credited on many of their freshman courses, having had the equivalent here. Our graduates have gone on to great success: one is a Kenan Fellow, another the editor of the University of Edinburgh newspaper, the oldest university newspaper in the world.

Again, the vision was that this school would be a model, the thinking being that some of the public schools would pick up on some of the practices here, see what worked, and take it to their curriculum and their classrooms. Leaders have to be willing to adapt. What we learned over this last decade is that everyone hasn't been picking up on this, making these additions and changes. So we've adjusted and are now really pouring all of that energy that we put into Cary Academy into the state's public schools. We've engaged ourselves and tried to take the best practices from here—teaching workshops for public school teachers, creative teaching projects—and share them with the public school systems. Our focus in the public schools is on the teaching of technology, and we've developed a Cary Academy team working with the Golden LEAF Foundation, the New Schools Project, the General Assembly, and the Friday Institute at NC State. We advocate the professional development of public school teachers, one-on-one teaching, and a computer for every child. And yes, we still see the Cary Academy as a model for education, one that can, has, and continues to offer innovative teaching and educational programs for use in North Carolina's public schools.

Dr. T. Ming Chu

A Teacher Willing to Be Taught

Chair emeritus of diagnostic immunology research at Roswell Park Cancer Institute, Buffalo, New York; early pioneer in using tumor cell products for the diagnosis and therapy of cancer

Having played a leading role in the development of the PSA test and prostate cancer research using tumor cell products for diagnosis of cancer, I'm very happy to acknowledge credit that is so deserved by my team. Although they were too numerous a group to name individually, their contributions were very important. I would like to emphasize that it was my pre- and post-doctoral fellows who played the most pivotal role in this research. These young students are the workhorses of a project like this and deserve credit for the results of what we call translational research, scientific discoveries that are translated into practical applications.

Prostate cancer is a malignant disease of older men, especially fifty-five years of age or above, which can kill mercilessly. In the 1960s and early '70s when I began this investigation, 75 percent of all prostate cancer was detected after it had spread into other tissues or organs in the body, or had metastasized. Fortunately, if prostate cancer is detected early, lives can be saved.

Now, as a result of our work, the prostate cancer can be detected by the PSA test as recommended by the American Cancer Society. With early detection there has been a dramatic change or shift in the results, with a 99 percent five-year survival rate for prostate cancer, and, combined with the treatment, prostate cancer is no longer the killer it was thirty-five years ago.

I have been very fortunate to see the success of my PSA research, and over the years, have met so many prostate cancer survivors, some well known like the actor Barry Bostwick, General Norman Schwarzkopf, and former U.S. Senator Bob Dole. Senator Dole has credited the PSA test for saving his life and has been an advocate of the test on national TV, shows like *Larry King Live*. The test alerted him to his prostate cancer in 1971. Later, he came to Buffalo. Before that trip, and I will always remember this, he said, "I look forward to shaking the hand of the man responsible for the test that saved my life." I was very pleased to meet him, as well as many regular folks, including ladies who have come to thank me for saving their husbands' lives or improving the quality of their lives.

So I feel great about all this, but I see this translational research in an intellectual sense as well. I'm very proud of what we've been able to contribute to important scientific knowledge. The key elements to this success were leadership, application of knowledge, and experience combined with determination and commitment.

I'm very happy to acknowledge that the education I received at NC State University also helped prepare me for this successful endeavor. My adviser and professor, Dr. Leonard Aurand, was a leader who saw potential in me as a student. It was his letter of acceptance to the graduate program that brought me from Taiwan to Raleigh, his students who shared their lecture notes when I was having so much trouble with the English language, and Dr. Aurand's recommendation to take quantitative organic analysis, a very tough biochemistry course, a course that gave me knowledge and confidence. My fellow students kept telling me not to take it, that I was going to flunk. But Dr. Aurand knew that this would test my scientific aptitude and did not require much English, and that all the work was in the chemistry laboratory. So I was successful while at NC State, and later at Penn State, where I received my Ph.D., I worked in an environment that provided me the fundamental scientific knowledge and the basic training in biochemistry that enabled me to extend my research into cancer immunology and its diagnostics and prevention. Today, when training graduate students and post-doctoral fellows, this experience comes to mind.

I recently read several books about the early navigation between Hawaii and Tahiti. About two thousand years ago, the Polynesians migrated from Bora Bora to Hawaii and they, of course, did it without GPS systems. They accomplished this navigation guided only by the stars and the waves and the swell of the ocean. This reminded me of the way I train my students. As the captain or leader, I point them in a direction, and they have to use their own navigation systems to find the answers. If they need an adjustment, then I will step in and set them on the right track. But it is their own navigation or skills that take them to the answers. I always tell my students on the first day of class that if they would like an A in this course, then they will have to teach me something that I don't know about that subject. To me, it is a fine way to show leadership and to train the leaders of tomorrow.

Dr. Jerry Punch

A Center of Influence

Well-known face in ABC and ESPN broadcasts of auto racing, serving as ABC and ESPN's lead announcer for 2008 NASCAR coverage; former play-by-play and sideline reporter for college football and basketball; trauma specialist and former director of emergency medicine and chief of staff at Coastal Communities Hospital in Florida

I remember a leadership moment that changed my life, one that assured me a career in medicine. Dr. Reinhard Harkema was a senior professor of comparative anatomy in the College of Agriculture and Life Sciences at NC State. And he was sort of the giant in that department in more ways than one; he was at least six-five, maybe taller. Dr. Harkema was just one of those people who always had a smile and a wink for everyone and came across as a very grandfatherly figure. I was maintaining an average that wasn't quite a 4.0 . . . but close. I was very aware that my parents were struggling in western North Carolina to make ends meet. My father worked two jobs, one in the day and one at night, and my mother worked in a school cafeteria. I realized that putting the financial burden of medical school on my family would be way too much for them. So I went to Dr. Harkema and said that I thought I should change my major from pre-med and get into pharmacy school. This would allow me to get that degree, generate an income sooner, and relieve some of the burden on my mom and dad.

Dr. Harkema looked me in the eye, then looked at my grades. He knew how hard I'd worked and he said, "Mountain Boy [he always called me Mountain Boy], you're not going to give up on your dream. You're going to apply to medical school and be accepted because I'm going to write you a letter. I have a whole drawer full of letters that I send out, some out of courtesy but I'm going to handwrite yours. And when you get into medical school, you and I are going to walk arm-in-arm down Hillsborough Street, and go from bank to bank until we have enough money to take care of medical school, so it won't be a burden on your mom and dad. I'm not going to let you give up on that dream."

That conversation must have lasted about an hour but, in a sense, this was a leadership moment. Because he made me feel so at peace with this decision and then, when I asked what I could ever do to repay him, he simply said, "Mountain Boy, when you graduate from medical school, here's what you can do. You know that stuff you make up in the mountains, well, just come by my office and bring me a jar of moonshine!"

I'd applied to UNC, Duke, and Wake Forest and was accepted to all three medical schools. I chose Wake because I'd be closer to the mountains and my family. Now, that moment with Dr. Harkema stayed with me my first year in medical school, and I really thought it would be something to walk into his office one day and present him with that little jar. Well, as it turned out during that first year at Bowman Gray, the dean of our medical school was scheduled to come to NC State to speak to Alpha Epsilon Delta, the national pre-medical honor society there. Typically, the dean selected a fourth-year medical student, an NC State grad, to go with him on these speaking engagements. Well, for some reason the student who was going to go with him had rotations in the hospital or something and couldn't go.

Now, as a first-year medical student I was like everyone else; we didn't have time to sneeze, we were that busy. But the dean saw me in the hallway the morning of this event, knew that I was an NC State graduate, and asked me to go with him to make this presentation. I had to rush home, shave, and shower and try to find the only sport coat I owned, the one I'd purchased just for my medical school interviews.

I gave the talk to the students, saying that a year ago I was sitting where they were sitting and that now, I was realizing my dream. When I said that, the part about living my dream, I looked up, and way up at the top of this big classroom was Dr. Harkema. So I stopped right there and told this group the story about this man who wouldn't let me give up my dream, and how much it meant to me, and how comforting it had been to me as I went through the challenges and stresses that come with medical school. I told them about Mountain Boy and the promise—the story about the jar of moonshine—and how I was going to thank him when I graduated from medical school. Well, I asked him to come down front and he did. I gave him a big hug and told those students what Dr. Harkema really meant to me and to so many students, that he was a great teacher but so much more. How lucky we all were to have someone like that, someone who genuinely cared about and provided for his students.

I guess it was a few weeks later that I got the shocking news that Dr. Harkema had been killed riding his bicycle on campus. I was devastated. But over the years, I've looked back thinking how serendipitous that moment was when the dean of our medical school needed someone on short notice to go with him to Raleigh. It gave me the opportunity to thank the man who would prove to be the most influential leader in my life. I was so saddened by his death and, of course, have always regretted that we never had that moment together . . . the one where Mountain Boy walked into his office and handed him that jar of moonshine.

Erskine Bowles

Good Policy, Good Process

*President, The University of North
Carolina; White House chief of staff,
Clinton administration; UN deputy special
envoy to thirteen tsunami-affected
countries in Southeast Asia*

My understanding of leadership goes back to my father, Skipper Bowles. When I was just a boy I remember going to a dinner over in Winston-Salem, and my dad was going to get some kind of prestigious award. He looked at the audience and then at my two sisters and me and said, "Thank you, but I don't want you to judge me based on what I've done. I want you to judge me on what my children do for others." Later we asked him what he meant by that and he said, "Look, I believe that the success that I've had and the good decisions I've made in my life are a reflection on the values I got from my parents and the good education that they provided me. I think the choices that you make will be similar, a reflection on your mom and me." My dad used to always talk about how in the old South when you went out to chop firewood for your own family that you'd always throw a few logs on the community woodpile. He'd say, "I want you all to feel that it's always important to add to the community woodpile."

So all of us—my sisters included—have, in our own distinct ways, tried to do just that, think about that night and what my father said in every leadership effort we've undertaken.

I've had numerous opportunities to lead, and for that I'm very grateful. Working as President Clinton's chief of staff, head of the Small Business Association, and then later as the UN deputy special envoy to thirteen tsunami-affected countries in Southeast Asia all provided unique experiences.

Over the years people have asked me about the balanced budget when I was chief of staff during the Clinton administration, wondering if that wasn't the proudest moment of my time in leadership in Washington. My response is, "Yes, in some ways, but my proudest moment was putting together a team that had sharp minds and not sharp elbows. We really focused on trying to move the country forward rather than to take some kind of partisan advantage. We did it by taking partisanship off the table, establishing trust on both sides of the aisle." But the part of the balanced budget story that I like the best is this: while we were balancing the budget we got twenty-seven billion dollars of new funding for health care insurance for five million poor kids. This was values-based leadership. While being fiscally responsible we were still investing in something that could really make a difference in the lives of the kids.

Leaders can't be afraid of failure. What we have to be is not afraid to try. It isn't always glamorous and glorious. Most people in Washington think that you have to spend your time focused on policy, but you can't have good policy without good process. Good leaders have to inspire people, make them take ownership in the policy and process. You can come up with the right idea but you have to have organization, focus, and structure to make it real or you're never going to get to the promised land.

When they offered me this job as president of The University of North Carolina in 1997, I couldn't take it. It was really the one job in public service that I wanted, because Bill Friday was my hero. But I'd just taken the chief-of-staff position in the White House. Now, in a lot of ways, I believe that I was lucky and the state of North Carolina was lucky, because I don't think I'd have done a very good job then. Good leadership can be very much about experience. Being chief of staff gave me an opportunity to run something really big and really public. It gave me a chance to deal with the media, which you have to do with this job, and an opportunity to deal with the legislature. So that was very important experience, very helpful. Working with Secretary General Kofi Annan and the United Nations with the tsunami effort taught me a lot about how to focus on coordination. This is really a big coordination job, because we have seventeen universities in the system. While traveling to every county in North Carolina as a candidate for the U.S. Senate, I met many of the people whom we serve. I think that helped me get it right on things like tuition in our university system. I'm always going to lead the fight to keep tuition really low, because it's so important for North Carolina people to be able to afford to get a college degree, important for them personally and for our economy. But a low tuition without a quality education would be of no benefit to anybody, so in holding revenue down we had to cut expenses. We chose to cut the university system's administrative budget by 10 percent, which I guess you might say was our effort to throw a few logs on the community woodpile.

General H. Hugh Shelton Leadership Center
NC State University
General H. Hugh Shelton
United States Army (R)
14th Chairman, Joint Chiefs of Staff

SECRETS OF SUCCESS
North Carolina Values-Based Leadership

DONORS

CHAIRMAN'S LEVEL

Chris Collins and John McNeill

Cline Cellars/Southern Vines, LLC

FOUR-STAR LEVEL

The North Carolina Agricultural Foundation, Inc.

College of Agriculture and Life Sciences, NC State University

THREE-STAR LEVEL

Cooke Realtors of Ocean Isle Beach, North Carolina